To Ann. - A Real Mother.-,

Reading this profound
epistle of advice should entertain
you in the Hospital and
send you home with new zest
for your brood.

affectionately,

Lila

THE COMPLETE BOOK OF ABSOLUTELY PERFECT HOUSEKEEPING

ELINOR GOULDING SMITH

The Complete Book of Absolutely Perfect Housekeeping

AN UPROARIOUS GUIDE FOR DISORGANIZED HOUSEWIVES

(WITH NEAT SOLUTIONS TO SLOPPY PROBLEMS)

Drawings by Roy Doty

HARCOURT, BRACE AND COMPANY • NEW YORK

For My Family
(*you can easily see why*)

CONTENTS

Contents

THE COMPLETE BOOK OF ABSOLUTELY PERFECT HOUSEKEEPING

Running the Household

(and running and running and running)

I hate to think of any woman finding it difficult to manage a home. It is, but I hate to think of it. However, the difficulties should merely add zest and challenge to a job that is stimulating, meaningful, varied —and utterly loathsome. Running the home requires many skills, a calm happy disposition, a little common sense and efficiency, and a good strong back. Anyone can learn, with a little practice, to do six things at one time and answer the door, too.

When you analyze it, it's really laughably simple. All that is necessary, actually, is to cook and serve three meals a day, do the marketing, the laundry and ironing, clean the house and make the beds, do the sewing and mending, painting and papering, a little simple plumbing and wiring, a bit of carpentry, some bookkeeping and gardening, and be relaxed, charming and well groomed at all times. Isn't it laughably simple? Now let's all sit down and have a good laugh over it.

There are several small obstacles to be overcome in being a successful housewife. They are—and we might as well face them bravely at the start—hunger, dirt, rubbish, breakage and wreckage, a tendency of things to get in the wrong places and a tendency of the right places to get filled up with the wrong things, the obstinacy of machinery, dust, chicken pox, runs in stockings, Howdy Doody, ashtrays, nasty tempers, alarm clocks, weeds, door-to-door salesmen, finger paints, clutter, litter, butter, batter, clatter, lint, fuzz, crumbs, cat hairs, garbage, leaks, fuses, cracks, creaks, chips, scratches, mold, scattering, shattering and spattering, husbands and small children. Now. When you look at it all squarely and honestly, don't you feel better? There's nothing like facing facts, no matter how dismal. They are dismal, aren't they?

A few simple general rules at the outset will be helpful before we go on to the more specific topics. The main thing to remember is never to try to do too much in one day. When you find yourself lying absolutely unconscious on the floor, rest there a few minutes before starting to wash all the Venetian blinds. It is sometimes possible to rest even while you're working, and it is important to learn this trick. For instance, you're on the top of a stepladder painting the kitchen ceiling and it's the end of a long hard day and you still have to bathe the children and you're

having six for dinner that night. Don't be discouraged. All you need is a moment's rest. As you bend down to dip the brush in the can of paint, lean on the ladder a moment, let your arms hang down and your tongue hang out and your hair droop. It is surprising what a moment's rest like that will do, if you really let yourself feel relaxed. You may even find that you have recovered enough energy and strength to get to the phone and call the ambulance all by yourself.

Of course when the telephone and doorbell ring, they do have to be answered and naturally this often presents a problem since they are most likely to ring when you're (a) shampooing your hair, (b) making hollandaise sauce, (c) getting in the car, or (d) wallpapering the attic bedroom. There is, however, a solution to every problem. Don't get rattled. Just keep in mind that nobody lives forever. One thing you might do is to put a telephone extension in every room in the house. Of course then you won't have enough money left to buy groceries, but perhaps you could eat in restaurants for a while? Or you can wait till one of your children is old enough to answer the phone for you. This is really the best solution except that you never will find out who Mr. Gwarfing was.

If you can afford a house all on one floor you are fortunate. Those who are less fortunate do have to go up and down stairs. It is important that you climb the stairs properly in order not to be tired out at the end of the day. The correct posture is head up, chin in, back straight, toes curled, fists clenched and teeth gritted. Breathe deeply. You may pant on the second trip and a little light gasping is permitted on the third. When carrying a heavy load, always try to balance it. For instance, if you have a basket of wet clothes under one arm, take the baby under the other. He's bound to be going somewhere anyway.

Efficiency is the real secret of success and happiness and efficiency means *planning ahead*, and thinking out every move to save time and effort. You can make every moment and every step do the work of two. Never move about aimlessly and empty-handed. It is foolish to climb a flight of stairs without carrying a few things with you. Remember that in a house things are always out of place and if you're on your way upstairs there are bound to be any number of things that are now downstairs and ought to be moved upstairs and vice versa. For instance, you're in your bedroom on the second floor and you're on your way to the kitchen. Stop and Think! Look about you to see what should be carried down with you. Do you need any blankets in the kitchen? No. Did you accidentally leave a bowl of Jello on the bureau that you've been meaning to put in the refrigerator? No? Well, never mind. Go down empty-handed. Maybe next trip you can be more efficient.

TWO

All You Could Possibly Want to Know About Food

(more, even)

The preparation of meals is of course about the most important thing that the housewife does, and causes, perhaps, more trouble than any other single phase of housekeeping. It includes the planning of meals, marketing, cooking, table-setting, dishwashing and collapsing.

The average family eats one thousand and ninety-five meals each year. This may sound a little discouraging, but, as in everything else, there are shortcuts. The most important shortcut in preparing and serving meals is The Restaurant. The judicious use of The Restaurant is a boon to the housewife as it saves hours of time. It is customary for the husband to pay for meals at restaurants, and therefore this also effects a considerable saving in grocery bills which you can show him proudly at the end of the month. He will be delighted with your thrift, especially as he will notice that he himself has run a little short.

A second very important shortcut in the serving of meals is The Can of Tuna Fish. I have known docile husbands to eat canned tuna fish for several years before consulting a lawyer.

However, there is a limit to the use of The Restaurant and The Can of Tuna Fish, so we may as well get on with the planning of meals. There are several things to remember in meal planning, and once you have grasped these major principles it is not really too difficult. You have only to keep in mind that each meal must be balanced in its nutritional elements, attractive in color, varied in texture, and as different as possible from the previous meal. It should make use of the butcher's specials, and it should not include too many complicated dishes or require too many serving plates.

The term "nutritional elements" may require some explanation for the novice housekeeper. There are several nutritional elements, and you must cram as many of them into every meal as you possibly can. They protect your family's health! youth! and vitality! Besides, they keep your teeth from falling out.

There are starches, Vitamin B^1, amino acids, Vitamin A, proteins, minerals (such as copper, iron, cobalt, and manganese), carbohydrates, Vitamin C, niacin, Thiamin, Vitamin K, Nicotinic Acid, coal tar, riboflavin and sugar (such as beet sugar, corn sugar, cane sugar, natural sugars, refined sugars, granulated, powdered, confectioner's, lumps, tablets and midgets). This list *must* be committed to memory and taken along with you when you go marketing.

A simple menu for a light family supper might start with Shrimps Rémoulade, Vichyssoise, Poached Salmon Mayonnaise with Capers, and for the main dish, a Canard aux Cerises Noires. A tossed green salad would be nice with this, and for dessert a Hazelnut Torte with plenty of whipped cream. Finish off with coffee and cheese and crackers and fruit. You can fill it out, if the family is very hungry, with celery and olives and lots of rolls. Of course this is just a suggestion to get you started. Now all you have to do is think up one thousand and ninety-*four* meals.

Marketing is time consuming and apt to be a bit strenuous and should, therefore, be kept to an absolute minimum. For an average family of four, with an average refrigerator, twice a week should be sufficient. I plan my marketing for twice a week, and it is seldom that I have to make an extra trip more than eleven or twelve times. Actually the most difficult part of marketing is Finding a Parking Place, and the next most difficult is Finding a Nickel for the Parking Meter. Of course if you double-park you eliminate both of these problems at one stroke, but this is a matter between you and your own conscience. Or, often, between you and the police.

The modern supermarket is a boon to the modern housewife, providing a dizzying variety of quality foods at low prices, and with a minimum of hazards. Naturally you will want to check all your supplies systematically and carefully before going to the market: cleaning supplies, staples, fresh fruits and vegetables, dairy products, baked goods, meats, frozen foods, and money. I like to keep a pad and pencil handy on my kitchen counter to jot down items that are getting low, but I can't because the children use it for their really important memoranda like addresses for send-ins on cereal boxes. It is helpful to keep on hand at all times one spare of things like salt and ketchup and mustard, and buy as soon as you open the spare. That way you never find yourself running out of staple goods. That is: you don't run out of them—you just can't find them. You *know* they're there. In fact you distinctly remember buying ketchup just the other day, but it absolutely is not to be found, and there is dinner on the table and the family raging with hunger, and no ketchup. The family grumbles, but eats. The next day when you go marketing you buy two bottles just to be on the safe side, and it is only when you try to find a place for them on the pantry shelves that you discover three more bottles of ketchup hidden behind some paper towels. This is too bad, because one of the things you have just dragged home, under the misapprehension that you were out of them, is four rolls of paper towels. However, there really aren't any paper napkins or mustard in the house, as you will shortly discover just when you're putting dinner on the table. Oh well. Better luck next time.

The supermarket will gladly carry your packages to your car for you, but there the service ends. They will not carry them home and put them away for you. So all you have to do now is carry the packages into the kitchen—and unwrap, wash, pick over, wrap up, scrub, pluck, sort, shell, remove stems, pits, bones, skins, fins, etc., put in bowls, put in the refrigerator, put on shelves in pantries, put in bread boxes, put on shelves in cupboards, and stack on floors in pantries and closets the things you have bought. You must also dispose of fourteen paper bags and three cartons, plus any number of little boxes and baskets and crates.

During this operation you will knock over in the refrigerator one opened can of tomato juice (the Large Economy Size) or (alternatively) one large bottle of grape juice. Grape juice is probably more likely because the stains are pretty nearly permanent. The door will ring twice (unless it is out of order in which case people will appear suddenly and frighten you) to announce the arrival of the plumber whom you called yesterday because the washing machine flooded the cellar, and to announce the arrival of a lady selling table linens. The children will arrive home from school, panting for their lunch, and an-

nounce that they have to get back early today because
of some major crisis which you cannot quite get the
hang of but it has to do with the first grades having
a teachers' conference or the janitor doing something
to the sixth grades' kick-ball tournament. *I* don't
know. The telephone will ring once more to ask if
you wouldn't like a freezer and six tons of food delivered right to your door at a twelve per cent dis-
count and again to ask if you wouldn't like someone
to come and mothproof your closets, and you say no
both times because you're an absolutely perfect housekeeper and absolutely perfect housekeepers say no on
principle. The plumber will come up from the cellar
looking doubtful and announce that he's going to turn
off all the water, a lady will come to the front door

to take a school census, and a man will come to the back door to demand knives to sharpen and umbrellas to fix.

But never you mind. You just keep right on putting away those groceries, or the ice cream will be slopping down the side of the table—oh, there it goes now. Well, never mind, you can always mop it up later, and perhaps when you go to the station to-night to pick up your husband you can buy some more.

There! Now you're all set. Your food is bought, paid for, carried home, and put away. Now all you have to do to it is cook it.

Cooking is not hard, and anyone who tries to tell you it is is just a trouble maker and don't you pay any attention to him. Or her. You keep on telling yourself that if everyone else can do it, you can too, and you keep right on telling yourself that while the hollandaise curdles, the rolls burn, the steak catches fire in the broiler, and the coffee boils over into the fried potatoes, the salad wilts and the cheese cake falls. After all, fire often gives steak a delicious flavor, and though curdling does not make your hollandaise look particularly attractive, it actually doesn't affect the taste at all. (Besides, it has three egg yolks and a quarter of a pound of butter in it, so you just go ahead and serve it no matter what anybody says.) And as for fallen cheese cake, we've eaten it often. It may be a little hard and a little dry and a little tasteless, but it's *good*.

There are several basic cooking procedures which you must understand at the start, and you must know how to apply them to the appropriate recipe and in the appropriate utensil. It wouldn't be nice, for instance, to boil lamb chops in a cake pan.

The main cooking procedures, without which you cannot get anywhere, are: Roasting, Baking, Broiling, Boiling, Poaching, Frying, Sautéing, Simmering, Steaming, Braising; and then slicing, dicing, icing, ricing, mashing, hashing, grinding, pounding, breading, dredging, beating, whipping, rolling, stirring, draining, straining, basting, tasting, toasting, testing, patting, punching, dripping and hoping. And you've got to get them all straight, too, or you're going to be in an *awful* mess.

Suppose your husband wants a soft-boiled egg for breakfast, and you don't know your basic cooking procedures. Suppose, in your ignorance, you broke the egg into butter in a hot frying pan. Boy, would *he* be mad.

"For Heaven's sake," he'd say, "that's not a boiled egg! That's a fried egg."

You would look at it, throw up your hands in astonishment, and say, "It *is?*"

Now some people are confused as to the difference between boiling, simmering and poaching. These are not hard to understand, really, as there is a *world* of difference between them. Simmering is cooking something very gently in water just below the boiling point. Poaching is cooking something *very* gently in water *just* below the boiling point, and the something is something more expensive than the something you simmer, and instead of just plain cooking it, you cook it with tender love and care, with your hands clasped under your chin, and you watch the timer *madly*. Boiling is altogether different. You boil any old thing. You just throw it into the pot with a lot of water. You can set the timer if you want, but who cares? That's boiling.

One trick to serving good meals is always to serve absolutely perfect coffee. You can even make your reputation as a cook if you are known for your perfect coffee.

"She is one miserable cook," they'll say, "even if she does make a good cup of coffee."

The best way to insure delicious coffee every time is to use the finest Arabian mocha, flown direct to you, freshly roasted, freshly ground, and freshly brewed with fresh water in a fresh glass coffee maker. If you can't manage this, you can always buy some instant coffee.

Then they'll say, "She is one miserable cook."

Another trick to remember is that an especially tasty appetizer before a meal will often throw people off guard and get them in a good mood before the meal starts. There is nothing more delicious than, say, a nice pot of fresh caviar to give a gala start to a little dinner, and it's easy to prepare. Even the novice cook can serve, with pride, fresh caviar. First you take your caviar, garnish with a few slices of lemon, some chopped egg whites and chopped egg yolks, finely chopped onion, and freshly made very thin toast, and presto! there you are all ready to serve your guests canapés that you can be proud you made *all by yourself.* Your husband will be amazed.

The main thing though is to start serving drinks as soon as your guests arrive. Don't let them refuse or all is lost. Keep pressing them to take more and if they say no, just keep filling their glasses behind their backs. Make the drinks stronger each time, and serve dinner a little later than is customary. Keep laughing gaily, and remind everyone that there's no hurry at all, and isn't it pleasant just to relax and take time to enjoy the drinks? Remark cheerfully that the main joy of having no help in the kitchen is that you can take as long as you like over your drinks, and nobody cares what time you eat. When they get to talking rather louder than usual and laughing a lot, *don't be misled*. It isn't time yet. Fill the glasses again. If anyone mentions anything about getting hungry, just laugh merrily and give him another drink. You must not serve dinner until the eyes are glazed, the speech slurred, the step faltering. *Then* you may announce that dinner is ready and graciously help your guests to the dining room. If they don't need your help, they aren't ready. Now, when you go ahead and serve, it can be chipped beef or boiled spare ribs or creamed hard boiled eggs—or even some canned pineapple and cottage cheese—*they* won't notice.

Never forget the hamburger, the frankfurter, the peanut-butter sandwich, the delicatessen, the pizza pie from a pizzeria, the chow mein from the nearest Chinese restaurant. These are healthful, appetizing, satisfying meals that even you can fix. Then of course there is the boiled lobster from the sea-food market, and the boiled shelled shrimp. And best of all, there is the Tartar Steak. If you omit the onions and the raw egg and the capers and the sardellen, it requires *very little* kitchen preparation and makes an excellent meal for any occasion. If your family tires of it, remind them that it is both nourishing and digestible, and next time put a sprig of parsley on it and tell them it's Steak Tartare.

Cook books have their place. If you don't know anything about cooking, buy one really good cook book and follow the recipes with the precision of a chemist. If you're a more advanced cook, buy several cook books, and use them all, but *never* follow the recipes. Alter the proportions, or change the ingredients, or add some ripe olives and a dash of wine—do *something*. When you're ready to be a really good cook, keep a large collection of cook books prominently on display so that everyone will see them and know that you're a gourmet, and *never consult them at all.* Make absolutely everything up out of your head. You may lose your husband, but at last you will have achieved truly creative cooking, which is marvelous because now you can use up all those scraps in the icebox.

Now that you know all about marketing and cooking, there is another phase to preparation of meals that is vitally important and often neglected, and that is Setting the Table. Naturally you try to provide variety and interest in your meals, and one way to heighten the pleasure of your family and guests is to serve them in interesting and unusual table settings. You can't expect your family to eat from the same old dishes every day. Can you?

You want, cleverly and cunningly, to use your table linens and china and glassware to set off the food. Suppose you have decided some night to have for dinner celery, halibut, rice, mashed potatoes, white bread, endive, white radishes, vanilla pudding, angel cake and milk. Wouldn't it be just *fun* to use the watermelon pink place mats?

Or suppose you're having chow mein and egg foo

yong. Why not try serving it in real Chinese rice bowls with chop sticks? Get some bamboo place mats, and to heighten the gay effect make a clever dragon out of an old kimono for the center of the table. Paper lanterns with candles in them would be really merry. A windbell tinkling at the open window, and perhaps a new teakwood table would complete the effect.

Setting a table, you see, is more than just putting out the necessary utensils. Here is your chance to use your ingenuity and your creative talent. Play with color! Let your imagination loose!

A big roast beef dinner on a cold winter night calls for handsome English bone china, real crystal goblets, and silver in a heavy traditional pattern. A dark red velvet cloth would be a happy choice, and for a centerpiece an old silver christening basin (any old silver christening basin you find around the house) heaped with white roses would add a nice touch.

A lighthearted French dinner—perhaps some Strasbourg paté followed by veal with mushrooms in white wine, a tossed salad delicately garlic scented, a soufflé, light as foam and golden crusted, for dessert—this calls for fragile Limoges china, silver in a stark modern design set off by tender pale green silk place mats just *touched* with gold thread, and why not serve the wine in square-footed glasses?

Now say, for the children's lunch, you're having ham sandwiches, milk and apples. How about some pottery dishes with a bright provincial pattern? Paint a gay wooden rooster for a centerpiece, and use homespun placemats trimmed with bright ball fringe to delight the small fry. Milk in Sandwich glass, of course, and serve the apples in a mellow old pewter bowl. (Any mellow old pewter bowl that you happen to have will do.)

The centerpiece sets the mood for your dinner, and gives you a chance to show off your clever artistry. Look around your house, your cellar, your attic, and your top closet shelves, for witty objects in which to arrange your flowers or fruits or whatever strikes your fancy. You'll find lovely old Meissen bowls you never dreamed you had. If you don't, you can always find one at an antique shop. Perhaps there's an old guitar which you could heap with lemons and limes for surprise effect. Or maybe you'll come across an old birdbath to pile with gay pineapples and nuts.

Don't be afraid to try unusual arrangements, and don't overlook the simple things. A bunch of carrots arranged with an old battered white enamel coffee pot might be just the thing! No, I don't think it is, at that. Try some children's blocks with pussy willow. That doesn't look too good either. Try—oh, hell. Go to the florist and get a dozen daffodils.

Now that we have completely covered absolutely perfect meal planning and cooking and table setting, we come to a subject that many women consider an unpleasant one. And that is, Washing the Dishes. I cannot understand why this is thought of as an unpleasant chore in so many many households. It is, after all, merely a matter of carrying the plates with their congealing grease, scraps of drying string beans, little surprising bits of garbage glued to their underneaths, particles of hardened egg, dried gravy, a few fish bones and some old bread crumbs to the kitchen sink, and removing these things. The purpose of Washing the Dishes is to remove all traces of the meal you have just finished, and it's a darn shame too, when you think how much work went into it.

There are as many ways of washing the dishes as there are people, ranging all the way from rubbing them in sand to putting them into an automatic electric dishwasher. I prefer the latter, myself.

An automatic dishwasher is truly a splendid machine, and will accomplish a great deal for you. However, keep in mind that there are certain things it will not do. It will not, for instance, clear the table for you, nor will it scrape the dishes, nor will it put the butter and cream and leftovers back in the refrigerator, and the bread in the breadbox, and get rid of the coffee grounds. Also, your husband will feel that having bought you a dishwasher entirely ends his responsibility in the matter of helping with the dishes, and he will never lift a finger again. Mine hasn't lifted a finger in eight years now, and it has become very stiff and swollen in the middle joint.

Here a pet comes into his own, and you may speed the work greatly by simply placing the dishes on the floor for a half hour or so, while the animal does his share. A dog or cat is the most useful type of pet for this work. Birds, goldfish and turtles fail to perform effectively at this task.

While the dog or cat is completing his chore, you have your cue to retire for a minute to make a phone call or powder your nose, thus leaving things squarely up to your husband and children.

If this ruse won't work—and it won't because they've all disappeared—you may as well make up your mind that you're in for it. You now have two courses open to you. You can go inside and watch television, or you can start applying hot water and soap to the right places. The technique is simple. The hotter the water and the stronger the soap, the quicker the job will be done, and the quicker all the skin will slough off your hands. The trouble with dishwashing is that if you do it slowly you'll miss Groucho Marx, but if you do it fast you'll break all the dishes. On the whole, though, the latter is by far the lesser of the two evils, and when your husband wonders why you're buying up so much china you can honestly reply that you need it.

Actually, it is my belief that most women are born knowing how to wash dishes, that, in fact, washing dishes is an involuntary act on their part—a compulsion. The important thing to learn is how to get that monkey off your back, and get along without washing dishes, and this is more a matter of character than skill. It takes a strong will to walk out of the kitchen and leave the dishes, but it *can be done*. It's a little like giving up smoking. The first few days hurt the most, and if the addiction is very strong, you won't even enjoy the television program. You'll keep thinking about the hardened egg and the wilting lettuce. But if you really *want* to overcome the habit, *you can do it*. Try chewing gum or take up knitting or nail biting. You'll be surprised at how soon you'll be able to walk out of the dining room without even clearing the table.

Once you have mastered this evil mania, you have but one more step to the final accomplishment—to be the last one down to the kitchen in the morning. A good wife and mother is the first one down in the morning to make breakfast for her family. But the absolutely perfect housewife is the last. By that time someone, a husband or a small boy, is bound to have grown hungry, cleared away last night's dishes and made breakfast. (If all they do is stack the dishes in the sink, never mind. Sooner or later a cleaning lady is bound to show up, or perhaps you could be sick for a day or so and your sister-in-law will come and do them.)

All you have to do is learn to take a little more time and trouble with your makeup in the morning. You may have to take it off and put it on again several times to get it just right. Give yourself a home permanent or put on fresh nail polish. You don't want to appear first thing in the morning looking like a frump, do you?

THREE

The Automaniacal Clothes Washer and the Perils of Ironing

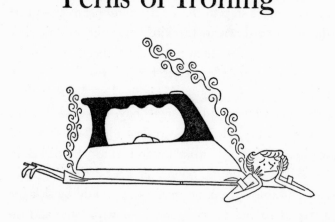

There is a primitive belief on the part of a great many otherwise sane women that clothes must be washed. Some atavistic corner of the mind carries a racial memory of the days when they crouched happily beside a stream and pounded clothing on rocks till it disintegrated. If you are one of these unfortunate women you must use every ounce of strength you have to fight this tendency. The fact is that if no clothing were ever washed at all it would last a great deal longer than it now does. Washing causes threads to slip, seams to open, belt loops to pull off, zippers to jam, collars to wrinkle, sleeves to pull out, ma-

terial to fray, hems to come down, skirts to sag, blouses to shrink, colors to fade, whites to yellow, and blacks to turn grayish. On the other hand, without any washing whatsoever, all that will happen is that the clothes will become very dirty. (Oh, very dirty. Especially the children's T shirts. They will accumulate quantities of gravy, ketchup, butter and ice cream, perhaps even a corn flake or two.) Now which do you prefer? To be colorful or clean?

If, after all this, you simply cannot control that savage impulse to beat your clothes to death, go ahead. Very few women in America today beat clothes on rocks. Hardly any even use a scrubbing board any more. And we need scarcely mention the clothes boiler which is as out of date as an immovable refrigerator shelf. Most women today use the Auto-maniacal Clothes Washer, either in Launderettes or in their own cellars. Some, who cannot afford the automaniacal washer, use just the plain ordinary washer (which does almost the same thing, but requires some hand labor in turning dials and knobs—very tiring).

The procedure is not difficult. You gather up the soiled clothing in a wash basket, you carry it down to the cellar, and you put it in the machine, being careful not to put colored things in with the white, wool with the cotton, or the stuffed mouse that one of the children left in his shorts' pocket. You plug in the machine, turn on the water, put in the soap and bleach, set the dials for the proper temperature and washing time, and go away. You should also make sure that the drain hose is hanging on the washtub and that the washtub drain is not full of lint, or your machine will empty itself on the cellar floor, and since the machine holds some twenty gallons of water and empties itself at least three times during its run, this is very poor housekeeping practice. When this happens, the sixty gallons of water must be mopped up and bailed out and this is very time-consuming, backache-making, and shoe-ruining. However, when it does happen, BE CALM. Screaming and kicking the wash basket to a pulp will not remove the water. See Chapter Eight, PLUMBING IS FUN! for further instructions.

Now it is obvious that an average family of four is going to have an awful lot of laundry unless you take steps. There are socks, bedspreads, guest towels, napkins, shirts, pillowcases, curtains, doilies, scarves, sheets, white gloves, sweaters, slip covers, white linen collars and cuffs, more socks, blankets, pajamas, pillow cases, and more socks, ALL DIRTY. It is apparent, therefore, that unless you do something to stem the tide you are going to spend most of your life galloping up and down the cellar stairs with laundry baskets. You won't even have time to create unusual centerpieces for your dinner table.

First, throw away all your curtains. This will not only save washing and ironing time, but also taking-down and putting-up time, mending time, shopping time, starching time, etc. Second, throw away all your bedspreads. This will save hours of bedmaking time. They're awfully shabby anyway on account of the cat pulling off all the fringe. Third, throw away all your table linens. They're old-fashioned. (See Chapter Two for Table Settings.)

You can't throw away all the clothing—at least not if you're going to go on living in the same neighborhood—but there are steps to be taken to cut down on the quantity. Every time you see one of your children taking a clean T shirt, slap his hand. Each time your husband takes a clean pair of socks, wince noticeably, and forget to use the sock stretchers. You might give up darning for a while, too. In time they'll catch on, all right. And you'll save hours of work.

There are some further aspects to laundry, and they are: starching, bleaching, rinsing and blueing. These are very professional, and, while not absolutely vital, do give a nice finishing. The techniques are not difficult, and the main thing is to read the labels on the bottles. You must be sure to bleach, starch and blue the right things. If you bleach the blue jeans they are not going to look right, and if you starch the socks they are going to be very hard to put on. The byword here is Caution.

One other common laundry problem is nice little wash dresses for nice little girls. There is nothing sweeter than a little girl in a nice fresh clean starched dress, with nice clean starched petticoats under it. This takes a lot of washing, soaping, bleaching, starching, ironing, scowling and frowning. But there is something to do about it and that is to raise them to be tomboys.

Once the clothes are washed, you have only to remove them from the machine, put them back in the basket, carry them from there to the line or dryer, hang them up or put them in, wait till they're dry, take them down, or out, put them back in the basket, carry them around some more, sort them, iron them, fold them, and put them away nicely in bureau drawers and closets. Then stand by and *dare* anybody to touch them.

We now come to ironing.

I understand there are some women who *do* iron. This is foolish. For fifteen years my home has been

a non-ironing laboratory in which I have proved, beyond a doubt, that you can live for an indefinite
length of time without ironing.

Take into consideration, nylon, dacron, seersucker,
corduroy, sweaters, knitted cotton, jersey, orlon, cotton plisse, fiberglas, crinkled cotton. Aren't those
enough materials for you? Are you so materialistic
that you absolutely can't live without smooth cotton,
silk, linen and rayon? If you are, then at least consider the dry cleaner and the laundry. Consider something. But don't lift that iron!

Perhaps you think you can do just a *little* ironing.
You think perhaps you might just iron one handkerchief. You plug in the iron and set up your ironing
board. You're a smart housekeeper, so you've provided yourself with an adjustable ironing board. You

set it at a comfortable height and get a chair so you can sit down while you work. You even provide yourself with a cigarette and an ashtray, perhaps a tall glass of iced tea to refresh yourself while you're waiting for the click that tells you that your iron has reached the proper temperature. You hum to yourself as you dampen the handkerchief nicely, and roll it up into a ball so it will be evenly damp. Perhaps you have a radio handy to entertain you while you work, or a book to read while you wait for the iron to heat. You're happy, calm, contented and relaxed. You are totally unaware of the imminent danger. *This is the most dangerous moment of all.* If you have any sense at all, that is if, instead of being an excellent housekeeper, you are an absolutely perfect housekeeper, you will now *unplug that iron*, quick, before it's too late. Click! Too bad. It's too late. You go ahead and iron the handkerchief. The handkerchief is just the right degree of dampness, the iron at exactly the right temperature, and it glides smoothly over the linen. It's sort of fun, isn't it? The wrinkles come out, the material gets beautifully smooth, you carefully even out the hems, stretching them a bit where they're puckered. And then you think, "Well, here now. The iron is nice and hot, the board all set up, while I'm at it, I'll just press that white blouse." So you get the blouse, and you dampen it nicely, and roll it up, and just then your eye falls on a pair of shorts, so you think well, while you're at it, you'll just do those too.

An hour later you're wilting over a pile of ironing.

The wash basket is filled with dampened waiting clothes, and there's another pile dripping off the end of the ironing board getting in your way. The pile of freshly ironed things, though grand in its way, is discouragingly small compared to the waiting mountain. The ice has melted in the iced tea, the cigarette has burned down, unsmoked, in the ashtray. Your hair falls dankly over your perspiring brow, your eyes are lackluster. Your back aches, your right hand (if you're a right-handed ironer) has a cramp which grips it firmly and permanently to the handle of the iron. You couldn't stop now even if you wanted to, and your husband will have to remove the iron from your

hand by force when he gets home. Your sunny disposition has soured, crow's feet and crepey neck threaten you, dry skin is attacking. You have long since pushed back the chair and stood at your work to hurry things up, and look out, your arches are falling. The gay little song on your lips has turned to a croak and a gasp as you PRESS and PRESS and TURN THE GARMENT OVER and PUSH and STRETCH and CREASE and FOLD and OPEN OUT and FOLD UP and PRESS and PRESS and WATCH THE SEAMS and TOTE THAT BARGE and GET THAT CORNER STRAIGHT and GET THOSE ENDS OFF THE FLOOR and—heavens! This is *not* absolutely perfect housekeeping at *all*.

Besides, you have now discovered, too late, that most of the things you have been ironing CAN NOT BE IRONED. The black things have developed a hideous shine, the white things have scorch marks, nylons have melted, wools have matted, linens have burned and orlons have disappeared altogether. The following things cannot be ironed at all: pleats, gathers, shirrs, smocking, armholes, waistbands, hems, plackets, collars, cuffs, sleeves or shoulders, darts, gussets, gores, godets, and ruffles. Never mind why, they just can't.

Also, that one little handkerchief that started it all is now a wrinkled, soggy mess—you used it to mop your dripping forehead and neck.

You may feel that the purchase of an ironing machine will help matters. You have beautiful daydreams about putting a wash basket full of wrinkled clothes next to the machine, plugging it in, and going off to the movies while the machine feeds the clothes into itself and feeds them out again, smooth and beautiful. You couldn't be wronger. Not only will it not feed the clothes gently and smoothly into itself, it will, even with you standing by pushing levers and pedals, snatch things out of your hands, crush them to its hot bosom, and press wrinkles *in* that you never even suspected were there. Besides, you will now have the illusion that your ironing is easier and faster, and you will go on and on to ever madder flights of ironing. Sheets, which you formerly used unironed or sent to a laundry, you will now feed into this hot maw, discovering, alas, that where you formerly spent three hours on ironing, you are now spending days, and that, worse yet, sheets are *too big* to be ironed. However, an ironing machine *will* entertain the children. They like seeing the thing go around and the little lights go on and off, so you might consider buying one as a toy, but don't ever try to iron anything with it. You know those demonstrations that show how to iron a shirt in two minutes? I tried it once. That was two years ago and I still have one sleeve to do.

So take warning before it is too late. Don't iron that handkerchief. And remember, the watchword is SEERSUCKER!

FOUR

Pros and Cons of Vacuum Cleaning

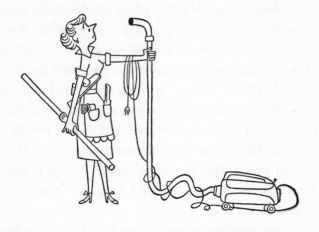

Dust is possibly the housekeeper's worst enemy and must be fought tooth and nail. It comes in through doors and windows, hot-air registers, children's pockets, and it comes out of mattresses, sofa pillows, last year's overcoats, books and closet floors. It must be got rid of. Right away. You never know when a dear and trusted friend or relative may drop in and run a white gloved finger along a baseboard behind the couch, and how would you feel *then?*

In order to dispose of dust scientifically, it is important to understand what it is composed of. It is chiefly made of soot, grit, grime, grease, cigarette ashes, sawdust, pocket lint, pollen, tobacco crumbs, spider web, bird feather, pine needles, cat or dog hair, human hair, blanket fuzz, and something mysteriously known as "house dust" which nobody knows *what* it is. All these elements are combined with smoke and grease from furnace, fireplace, stove broilers, french-fried potatoes, etc., and are then deposited on Venetian blinds, lampshade ruffles, hat boxes on the back of closet shelves, window mullions, old rubbers in the hall closet behind the unused tennis racket, and the rigging of your husband's model ships. Some housewives make matters worse by bringing into the home articles which not only *catch* dust, but actually *give it off themselves*, such as carpets, angora sweaters, fur coats, etc. These women can lighten their burden of housework by getting rid of all such articles immediately.

There are a great many weapons in everyday use against this major household enemy. There are dust rags, carpet sweepers, wet mops and dry mops, clothes brushes, push brooms (but no pull brooms), stiff brooms, soft brooms, Venetian blind slat brushes, oil mops, scrubbing mops, scrubbing pails, mop wringers, dust pans, trash baskets, ashtrays, polishing cloths, sponges, and scores of others, like the corner of the bath towel that happens to be in your hand when you just happen to notice the dust on the window sill in the kitchen. And of course, there is the vacuum cleaner, with its upholstery tools, brushes, and crevice attachments. The crevice attachment is very important—if there is one thing any house has plenty of, it's crevices.

Before we take up Vacuum Cleaning, its Pros and Cons, let us consider the other methods at our disposal. Mops, brooms and brushes do an effective job of removing the dust from where it is. It then rises in the air in a cloud, and settles slowly down, often, with luck, in an *entirely different place*. Naturally, this depends to some extent on air currents and weather conditions, but if you have the right kind of drafts you may be quite successful in transferring all the dust from, say, the floor to the tops of the bookcases or the piano keys. You can then stand back, and admire your clean floor. You can always get at the piano keys tomorrow. Meanwhile you can play the phonograph if you must have music.

Dust cloths are another effective measure in removing dust from picture frames, lamp bases, carved table legs and bric-a-brac, but in this case not all of the dust is transferred to another part of the house. Some of it remains on the cloth itself, which must then be washed out. In the process of washing out the cloth, a good deal of the dirt then remains in the sink or basin, and this must then be scrubbed out with a different cloth and some scouring powder, and a considerable part of the dust is then rinsed down the drain and *permanently out of the house*. However, don't be too optimistic. It isn't all out. Some of it now remains in the scrubbing cloth, which must still be washed out.

A broom and dust pan will pick up a good part of the cigarette ashes, candy wrappers, chocolate Oreo crumbs, apple cores and other ordinary floor dirt, but of course as you sweep it into the dust pan, some gets into the cracks (or crevices) between the floor boards, some sticks in the bristles of the broom, and some gets *under* the dust pan. Repeatedly retreating with the dust pan is a poor defense as sooner or later you back into a wall or chair. The dust pan is emptied into a waste basket, but note that it can only be partially emptied as there are always some *sticky bits*. The waste basket is then carried outside where it is emptied into a large trash can, and again there is some residue remaining in the waste basket. This can then be washed out with a scrubbing cloth, which is then washed out in a laundry tub or wash basin or kitchen sink, and this must then be scrubbed with that same old scrubbing cloth, and the scrubbing cloth washed, and so on and so on and so on.

Meanwhile, don't give up. Some of your dirt *is* out of the house, in the trash can. Tomorrow morning the sanitation men will come with their truck, dump your trash into a big carton and *carry it away*. Of course, in carrying it away, some of it falls out of the carton and gets strewed along the driveway, where it can once again easily be retrieved by children and brought back into the house. The part that is carried away on the truck is taken to the town incinerator where it is burned. Isn't that *good?* It is then borne along by the breeze, in the form of fine ash, and comes into your house through the doors and windows, hot-air registers, children's pockets and comes out of mattresses, sofa pillows, last year's overcoats, books and closet floors, and for Heaven's Sake, do you have to start all over again?

Yes, you do.

Now before we come to the subject of *Relief From Dust*, we will take up the vacuum cleaner. On second thought, let's leave it there. It's all dusty, and the wire's in a terrible tangle. Let's just talk about it.

The vacuum cleaner is the most efficient dust remover at the housewife's disposal, and a really good machine is certainly worth having. Some vacuum cleaners just clean carpets, but many of the newer models will clean absolutely anything, having an assortment of attachments for every kind of cleaning problem. (There are even some attachments for problems that haven't come up yet.)

The vacuum cleaner, as you may know, actually sucks up the dirt and dust and catches it all in one place. The newer models catch it in a paper bag which is easily disposed of, or in a metal container from which it is neatly poured into a paper bag. In either case, you can start it on its way to the incinerator much faster than by any of the methods we have already discussed, and you can therefore expect to see it drifting back into your house through the doors and windows, hot-air registers and children's pockets within a day or two. Those who cannot afford these fine new models can still do an excellent job with the older types. The only difference in the older models is that the dirt is caught in a cloth bag which is then simply emptied onto a piece of newspaper spread out on the floor for that purpose. You hold the bag tight with the sides of your feet, and shake. You then shift the bag to another place on the newspaper and shake again. It doesn't matter how many times you do this, as there is always more. It is then a simple matter to replace the bag in the machine and fold up the— WHO OPENED THAT FRONT DOOR?

However, there is much to be said for vacuum cleaning. While the vacuum cleaner is going, you won't hear the telephone or the door bell, and you will thus be spared many wasted hours of saying no to salesmen who are trying to sell you more mops and brooms and brushes, or salesmen who are trying to sell you quieter vacuum cleaners. You won't hear the cat, who has been chased up a tree by a dog and is mewing piteously, and you'll save lots of time not getting out a ladder and helping her down. Let her get down by herself. She went up by herself, didn't she? You won't hear the children throwing marbles down the stair well, and if you choose the proper time for your vacuum cleaning, you may even not hear Howdy Doody. Something, somewhere in the house is making a flood (see Chapter Eight) and you'll save mopping-up time as you won't find out about it till tomorrow.

On the other hand there is a great deal to be said against vacuum cleaning. It has a great deal of wire, far too much to be coiled up neatly, yet never quite enough to reach the other end of the room. The hose has a way of coming unattached just as you were about to get that cigarette butt that's been under the coffee table for weeks now. And most important of all, vacuum cleaning can get to be a bad habit that is very hard to get rid of. Some women become positively addicted to vacuum cleaning, and then they are very hard to get rid of.

On the whole, the safest policy in the removal of dust is *moderation* and tell your mother-in-law to keep her hands off your baseboard. And remember, dust on table tops is nice and makes an excellent place for the little tots to start their first arithmetic studies.

Now then, we come at last to the relief from dust which I promised in an earlier part of this chapter.

There are two very fine ways of getting rid of the problem of dust.

The first is to air condition the entire house, seal shut all the windows and doors, put mineral oil on the filters, and then sit back and put on weight. You've been looking a little peaked lately anyway.

The second method, equally effective, and also guaranteed to be in keeping with absolutely perfect housekeeping practice, is to call in a really reliable firm of painters and paperhangers and have the entire house done over. This will be very refreshing to the whole family and will entirely rid the house of dust and dirt and cobwebs. Have the floors scraped first, and while you're at it you might as well send all the furniture out to be reupholstered and order some nice new carpets. Don't forget to call the electrician and put in all new lighting fixtures. And while the work is being done, why don't you all take a nice trip somewhere? Canada might be fun.

FIVE

Plain Facts About Bureau Drawers

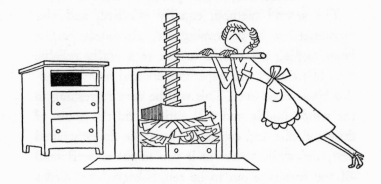

The thing nobody understands about bureau drawers is that they are not expansible. Their cubic capacity cannot be changed by prayers, hopes or burnt offerings.

This law applies with equal truth to all drawers—desk drawers, bureau drawers, kitchen drawers, etc.—and is easily demonstrable in a few simple experiments for which no expensive laboratory equipment is needed. For example, purchase a package of air-mail envelopes (easily obtainable at small expense at any neighborhood stationery, cigar, or chain store) and attempt to place it in the middle desk drawer.

Another good experiment is to obtain (from any hardware or home-furnishings store) a potato masher and open the top drawer in the kitchen cabinet. Do not attempt to place the potato masher in the drawer. Make your observations in repeated experiments, and write up the results in your laboratory handbook. Then return the potato masher to the store for a refund. Tell the man it doesn't work.

A third suggested experiment, and perhaps the most interesting of the three, is the following: Obtain a handkerchief (these are easily found in the hems of old coats whose pocket linings have deteriorated), have it freshly laundered, pressed and folded neatly, ready for use. Take the handkerchief (being careful not to disturb the folds) in the left hand, and attempt to open the top bureau drawer. (This may be a little difficult due to *warping*, which is the unfortunate result of having left the adjacent window open during a heavy snowfall. Or it may also in some cases be due to attempting to open the drawer with one hand, and firmly *wedging* the drawer in the bureau at an angle. However, the most frequent cause of the difficulty is an *unseen obstruction* within the drawer. What *can* it be?) Any of these difficulties can be overcome, however, with sufficient effort. A good sharp pull will often succeed in the case of *warping* or *wedging*. In the case of the *unseen obstruction* it is usually possible to pull the drawer open about a half inch; an exploratory index finger inserted in the space will often reveal the cause of the trouble. (If it is a new patent-leather handbag you can just go ahead and yank the drawer open by bracing your feet and pulling. You needn't worry—the handbag is already ruined. However, should the obstruction prove to be a leather belt that has somehow uncoiled itself, it is often possible to extract the belt through the crack, and then proceed to open the drawer in the usual way.*) Once the drawer is fully opened, you may (still holding the handkerchief in the left hand) proceed to pick up from the floor the handkerchiefs, scarves, etc., that came out with the belt, and replace them in the bureau drawer. Stir the contents of the drawer thoroughly with a rotary motion until some things which have been missing for years appear at the front. (Oh boy! My eyeglasses!) Many students find it beneficial to repeat this experiment, working down from the top to the bottom drawer, as the results are so unpredictable. If difficulty should arise in opening the bottom drawer, it is often helpful to remove the middle drawer entirely, provided you are properly shod. If you are still holding the handkerchief in your left hand (which you will be) you may now replace it in the old coat pocket until further needed.

It sometimes happens that a bureau drawer which opened with relatively little effort cannot be closed at all due, usually, to a too vigorous stirring of the contents. In this case it is most advisable to place certain items in the top drawer of your husband's bureau. In order to do this, of course, it will first be necessary to remove from *his* top drawer several ties,

*Actually it's not a handbag *or* a belt. It's really an empty box that seemed too good to throw away. (You can throw it away now, though.)

mufflers, gloves, old passport folders, his spare glasses, etc., and stuff them quietly in a trunk in the cellar. This is called Storing Things for the Winter, or Storing Things for the Summer, as the case may be. It will often be found to be unnecessary to mention this matter.

The law of the non-expansibility of drawers, or Smith's Law, must be demonstrated repeatedly, for although it may appear simple it is remarkably difficult for many people to grasp. Husbands, particularly, are notable for their inability to understand this basic law of physics. "For God's sake," they are apt to remark from time to time, "just *look* at these bureau drawers."

Take my advice and don't.

SIX

The Child
from One to Forty

The raising of children causes more difficulties than all other phases of housekeeping combined, including cleaning out the refrigerator. But two simple rules are the key to this whole problem.

Rule 1. WHATEVER YOU DO, YOU'RE WRONG ANYWAY, and

Rule 2. LET THE ANIMAL KNOW FROM THE VERY FIRST THAT YOU ARE HIS MASTER.

Commit these rules to memory at once and use them as often as possible.

It is a common belief that all children grow up to be either (a) criminals or (b) neurotics. This is not necessarily true as is evidenced by the fact that some children grow up to be policemen and some grow up to be psychoanalysts.

The modern mother fears the neurosis as her mother feared the germ. It is easy enough to define "germ" (horrid crawly little animals that are seen through microscopes) but it is not so easy to pin down a neurosis. What exactly *is* a neurotic personality? It is hard to find the fine line between mental health and neurosis, but if you, for instance, find it impossible to sleep at night out of terror that a little green man with a death-ray machine is going to come out of the closet, even the layman can detect that you are in trouble.*

It often seems to the new mother, as she wearily arises from her warm bed at two o'clock in the morning of a January night to feed a howling baby, that the first year or so is the hardest. Not at all. The first year, though beset by difficulties, is by all odds the easiest. Wait till he's two and pulls all the lamps off the tables. Wait till he's three and draws on the living-room walls. Wait till he's six and won't touch any meat that has a speck of fat on it. Wait till he's nine and hasn't learned to read yet. Wait till he's thirteen and wants to learn to drive a car. Wait till he's nineteen and wants an extra fifteen dollars for flowers and taxis for some girl he wants to take to a dance. Wait till he's twenty-three and all the other boys have

*In the event that you *are* in this trouble, the most sensible thing to do is to call the police immediately, and have them de-activate the death-ray machine.

[57]

good jobs as dentists and typesetters and television announcers, and HE wants to be an artist yet. Wait till he's twenty-eight and married and can't meet his mortgage payments. Wait till he's thirty-three and you have to be a baby-sitter for three grandchildren with head colds. Brother! You go back to that two o'clock feeding, and *like* it.

You will notice that the times when babies eat are called "Feeding Times." Not "eating times" or "meal times." This is significant. It means, quite simply, that at certain times of the day food is shoved into the baby whether he likes it or not in order to insure a proper gain in weight. THIS IS NOT ABSO-LUTELY PERFECT CHILD RAISING. It is obvious that as the baby cannot walk yet, *you* are going to have to carry him about. Your goal, there-fore, is to *keep his weight down* until he learns to stand on his own feet.

Another important element in the care of the baby is something euphemistically known as "changing the diaper." What this euphemism really means is chang-ing the diaper, shirt, gown, wrapper, blanket, sheets, bed pads and bootees* (if any).

One problem that causes many new mothers a great deal of distress is *crying*. All young mothers *do* cry, especially when the callous father has unthinkingly breathed on a freshly sterilized vitamin dropper. (Or when the ninety diapers that the diaper service sent

*Bootees are little foot garments whose function is to provide the grandmother with easy knitting. Bootees do not have to be terribly well-fitting.

are all used up by Thursday, and the diaper man isn't coming again till next Tuesday.)

When the baby cries some authorities say that he is just exercising his little lungs and should be ignored. However, this is utter nonsense as you cannot ignore a baby's cry at four o'clock in the morning with the telephone ringing every two minutes because the neighbors can't ignore it either. Other authorities say that when the baby cries, he has a good reason. And all you have to do is find out what the reason is. Could he be hungry? No, he couldn't. You just fed him an hour ago. Could his diaper (shirt, gown, wrapper, etc.) need changing? Try that. No, that wasn't it. Could he have a bubble? No, that wasn't it either. Could he perhaps just want to be turned over? Yes! That was it! What a piece of luck! Now you can go back to bed, and snuggle deliciously under the covers and—no, that wasn't it after all. Perhaps he'd like a little light in his room? No, that wasn't it. Could he be too hot? Could he be too cold? Would he like a stuffed animal in his crib? No-o-o. Would he like you to bounce him up and down on your knee and sing "This is the way the farmer rides," to him? Yes! That was it all the time! And now it's six o'clock and time to feed him again anyway. Oh well. Maybe you can sleep tomorrow night.

Some pediatricians recommend feeding the baby every four hours by the clock whether he likes it or not, while others insist on the newer "demand feeding." This latter is an excellent method except that from the very beginning the child gets the upper hand which is very contrary to Rule 2. However, don't forget Rule 1. It is a fact, moreover, that many mothers and babies often survive both methods and the babies grow up enough to develop feeding problems.

You can easily tell when a feeding problem has arisen by the following symptoms: (1) The child won't eat anything but Three Musketeers Bars. (2) The child won't eat anything but mashed potato. (3) The child will eat anything but mashed potato. (4) The child will take spinach, but only by hair. (5) The child will eat blanket fuzz, cat hairs, bathrobe sash tassels and dimes, but refuses lamb chops (rib and loin). (6) The child will eat absolutely nothing at home, but absolutely anything at the neighbors'. (The solution to this one is obvious; don't forget to pack his toothbrush and galoshes.)

Should a feeding problem arise, there are two things you can do. One is to make him eat the liver even if it makes him sick and tell him it's good for him, in which case he will never eat liver as long as he lives, or, you can give in to his whims and simply never offer liver, in which case he will never eat liver as long as he lives.

However, don't despair. I know one man who has lived a healthy normal life for forty-seven years while subsisting entirely on a diet of dry puffed wheat, and my own husband has lived for years on a diet of hors d'oeuvres and, except for the chicken pox, has maintained excellent health.

When the child learns to crawl and creep, or even, Heaven help us, to walk, he needs constant watching. If you turn your back for one second he will try the tablecloth trick and it won't work, or he will light all the burners on the stove without using one match. Therefore, if you are to get any curtain-ruffle ironing done at all, it is imperative that you set aside a certain period of the day when the child understands that he must remain alone in his play pen and play with his little wooden toys with rounded corners and non-poisonous paints. You should be firm about this. You might give him his own little clock to watch to help him pass the time. A good time for this quiet play would be from eight in the morning to six in the evening. Some children protest at first with remarkable strength, some even going so far as to turn quite purple, but REMEMBER RULE TWO. At six o'clock you may release him, give him some graham crackers and milk, and then tuck him up for the night in his crib.

Most cribs and play pens are constructed with strong slats around the sides, but some particularly active little children do manage to escape. In this situation you might consider putting bars across the top of the little cage—er crib—as well. Then he will be really safe. And you, too.

At about age three, the normal, healthy child develops a nasty tendency to litter. No matter how many cartons of rubbish you carry out of his room, it is still filled to the window sills with his treasures and you

need alpenstock, rope and axe to fight your way to his
bedside to tuck him in at night. Sometimes a long
heart-to-heart talk, in which you point out to him
how difficult it is to clean his room, how untidy it
looks, and how much he'll enjoy being able to use
his desk and bed again, may bring about a complete
change of heart and effect a thorough clean-up. However, it probably won't. When that doesn't work, a
little honest bribery is often effective, with the prom-
ise of all the Good Humors he can eat as the proffered
bribe. If he's a little older try five dollars. If he's
older still, try a new Cadillac. When all else fails,
REMEMBER RULE TWO and crack the whip.
This may help so much that you'll actually be able to
make your way across the room to kiss him good

night. Of course by now he just may not feel like kissing you good night, in which case you were probably right after all—he *is* getting neurotic.

When the child is somewhere between the ages of one and twenty-five it occasionally happens that a *second* child is born to the same parents. (Sometimes this is followed by a third, fourth, fifth, sixth, and even twelfth child—but this is such very careless housekeeping practice that we won't discuss it here.) When this happens, the second child, be it male or female, is technically known as a sibling. This is far more technical than calling it a brother or sister. This should be clearly understood before we go on to the next point. With the arrival of the sibling, usually at an inopportune moment, there also arises a new situation which is called SIBLING RIVALRY. Translated into terms which the layman can easily understand, this means, simply, that the two siblings hate each other on sight and try, by any means at their disposal,* to kill each other. This should be prevented at all costs as it is *against the law*. With the arrival of sibling rivalry there arises still another situation involving the mother, in which she feels that if she is forced to referee one more quarrel over whose turn it is to use the pencil sharpener she will take the next tramp steamer bound for Sumatra and devote the rest of her life to growing hemp. This is known as being *at the end of her rope*. However, should the father intervene by declaring that it is *his* turn to use the pencil sharpener, the sibling rivalry may resolve

*(bicycle-tire pumps, Venetian-blind cords, etc.)

[63]

itself by turning into an Oedipus Complex, which, however, is even normaler. Some parents try to avoid sibling rivalry by the purchase of *two* pencil sharpeners, but as one of the pencil sharpeners is a prettier color than the other, this is usually an ineffective measure. On the whole, probably the best bet for the mother is to leave home after all until the whole thing blows over.

During the course of the child's development, one problem recurs with increasing frequency, and the services of an excellent pediatrician, child psychologist, nose and throat surgeon, orthopedist or orthodontist will be of little help. This is a problem you and your husband will have to face all by yourselves. Money. At first the child doesn't cost too much as you can usually borrow a crib and a car seat and a play pen. But as he, or as luck may have it, she, gets older, he is going to want a rocking horse. Then he is going to want a kiddie car, then a scooter, then a tricycle, then stilts, then an Irish Mail, then roller skates, then a bicycle, then ice skates, then a motor scooter, then an old second-hand car, and then a

Thunderbird. And then what are you going to do? You haven't even finished the payments on the old Plymouth yet. Well, there is no problem to which there is no solution. Try borrowing from your brother-in-law. Or perhaps you could get a second mortgage on the house?

When there are children in a household, the subject of SEX and the far more complicated subject of SEX EDUCATION are bound to come up. Many parents believe it is their duty to answer the child's questions frankly and honestly, while others think the child has more fun finding it out for himself. In any case, by the time the child is twenty-five or so, he is bound to have noticed that there are *no storks* in the Western Hemisphere, and will have figured out for himself that this method of propagation is used only in Northern Europe, where the customs are very old-fashioned. Any attempt from this point on to keep the truth from him is likely to fail.

As the child gets older and older, you may find that he seeks your advice less and less frequently. But in this case, REMEMBER RULE ONE, and give it to him anyway. Criticize his clothes, his friends, his haircuts, his choice of a career. And after he's married criticize his wife's housekeeping, the furniture, and the way they raise their children. You are his mother, and don't let him forget it. Remind him of all the sacrifices you made for him. Remind him how faithfully you gave him his vitamins and darned his socks. And now you're entitled to *some* fun, aren't you?

SEVEN

Let's Interior Decorate!

Your home needs interior decorating. Right this minute your slip covers are shabby, your paint is dingy, your wallpaper is peeling, your rugs are threadbare, the upholstery is coming apart where the cat sharpens her claws, and the furniture was nothing much to start with anyway. Aren't you *sick* of it? I am.

You should understand before you undertake any decorating that there is no such thing as just a little decorating. You can't even slip cover that messy looking arm chair just to tidy things up till you can afford to do the whole room, because that one new slip cover will make everything else look worse than ever. Once you start picking out one piece of material to slip cover that chair, you are *through*. You might just as well start now to choose the new wallpaper and the new carpet and shop for furniture and lamps, except possibly that one lamp that you bought last spring that's still pretty good—but no-o-o, it probably won't look right with the new love seat after all. Better store it in the attic for now. It may come in handy some day for one of the children's rooms or better still, for some charity bazaar. It would be ideal for that.

So you tell your husband that you're going to do the whole house over, and then you go and cash in the bonds you were saving for the children's education. They won't mind. They don't like school much anyway. Get them a library card if they fuss.

Many women are frightened of interior decorating and fail to take advantage of this glorious privilege which is their birthright. It is even their *duty*. They are alarmed by words like Regency, Sheraton, French Provincial, Antique Satin, Eighteenth Century, etc. But there is really no need for anxiety as these terms require no knowledge at all.

Regency, for instance, refers simply to a period in French history (1715-1723) when Philip, Duke of Orleans, ruled for Louis XV (who invented a style of furniture known, aptly, as Louis XV). Or maybe it refers to a period in England (1811-1820) when George, Prince of Wales (afterwards George IV) was regent for George III (who was the man who put a tax on tea and caused a Revolution, thus putting an end to Colonial furniture and inventing Federal). The reason I happen to know so much when you don't know anything at all is that I have an unabridged dictionary at my side, and as it is not being used to press cucumbers today, I can look all these interesting things up in it, thus saving you endless trouble and making you an absolute expert on furniture styles. At any rate, to get back to Regency, you can be perfectly certain that it does not refer to any period in American History, because here the president is generally old enough to do his own work. Besides, European kings seem to have cornered the market on naming trends in design and except for McKinley (who named the gingerbread house) our presidents have failed miserably in perpetuating their names in this manner. This is what comes of having commoners in high position. As for Regency furniture, I would advise against it for you. You wouldn't like it. So if the salesman says, "How about this nice Regency sofa," you just say, "I don't think so, thank you." It has tassels, and they'll fray when the cat plays with them.

Now Eighteenth Century refers to the Eighteenth Century. (You see how this book is full of information you could never find elsewhere?) This is the period from 1701 to 1800, although some people mistakenly suppose that it refers to the period from 1700 to 1799. Some people even think it refers to the period from 1801 to 1900, or worse yet, 1800 to 1899. These people should not attempt any interior decorating as such attempts can only end in failure.

American Colonial (so called to differentiate it from Spanish Colonial or Dutch Colonial) is the term by which we call the furniture made in the United States before it was called the United States. At that time there were only the thirteen original colonies, chiefly composed of Virginia and Massachusetts. Now Colonial furniture, like French Provincial, might be anything from a three-legged milking stool hacked out by a farmer's small boy who wanted to sit down while he worked, to the most exquisite highboy. Or sometimes lowboy, depending on whether it was high or low. "Boy," as used in terms like highboy and lowboy does not, however, refer to this same farmer's boy who made the milking stool. To tell you the truth, I don't know *who* it refers to. Some people think it is a corruption of "bois," the French word for "wood" but this is really *too* far fetched. Actually, the safest thing here is to forget the whole miserable mess and just call it a "chest." Then you can't go wrong. I don't think you'd want Colonial furniture anyway. The real stuff is far too expensive, and the imitations far too cheap.

Luckily for us there wasn't too much furniture around until the Eighteenth Century. The first few centuries there were mostly only Romans who just had some divans to lie around on, and after them came the Dark Ages during which the people were too ignorant to know about trends in decorating and didn't bother much with furniture at all. They just threw rushes on the floor and called it home. I wouldn't worry about it though. You probably wouldn't like Eighteenth Century furniture. It's mostly dark polished woods, and shows the dust terribly.

French Provincial refers to furniture made, as you might have suspected, in the Provinces of France, and is generally made of fruitwood. (Such as apple, pear, peach, plum and banana.)

Hepplewhite and Sheraton sometimes confuse the novice interior decorator, but here again there is nothing in any way frightening about them. Hepplewhite and Sheraton were a pair of popular English furniture designers, similar to Gilbert and Sullivan, or Fortnum and Mason. I don't think you'd particularly like Hepplewhite *or* Sheraton.

Jacobean is a term designed to confuse the unwary as it has nothing to do with anybody called Jacob. It has nothing to do with Jack and the Beanstalk either. It does, however, have to do with the period of the reign of James the First of England (1603-1625), and why it is called Jacobean rather than Jamesian is anybody's guess. Some guessers guess it has some connection with the French "Jacques" or even the Latin "Jacobus," meaning James, but that is altogether too etymological and philological for a style that isn't really suitable for you anyway. You wouldn't like Jacobean. It's too heavy.

Victorian brings us once again to safe ground, as it does have to do with Queen Victoria, and not, as you might have feared after seeing some of it, with Ivan the Terrible. Victorian furnishings are very curly and puffy. You wouldn't want them. The children would catch their roller skates in the fringe.

Then there is William Morris, who invented the Morris chair, the Morris dance and the Morris Plan. There's Chippendale, Biedermaier, and Paul Mc-Cobb. And of course Adam, Queene Anne, Russel Wright, Paul Revere and many many others. I don't think you'd care too much for them though. Other furniture styles include Empire, Renaissance, Italian Provincial, and lots more. Why don't you look them up in some good book on the subject?

Perhaps after all you *should* just slip cover that chair and let the rest go for now?

Fabrics are no more difficult than furniture periods, and besides, usually the salesman will say, "How do you like this antique satin?" or "Do you prefer this chintz?" or "Would you perhaps care for a fine English linen?" If you're stuck, and you haven't the least idea whether it's burlap or brocatelle, you can always just say, "I don't care for the color of this," or "I love the texture of that." You might even say, "It's nice, but it won't go with the fringe on the lampshade on the little table by the other chair." If anyone mentions galloon or gimp, which heaven only knows what they are, leave at once and go to another store where they talk English.*

On the whole you can be perfectly safe if you stick to texture, as that is the *basis* of decorating today, and the most important word to use. You might also

*Look for a sign on the window that says, *"Ici on parle Anglais,"* or *"Aquí se habla Inglés."*

throw in something about tonal values. (This is a high-toned way of talking about light and dark, but don't worry—the salesman doesn't know *that*.) There is also mohair (itchy), velvet (dusty), and brocade (frays), but you needn't worry about them. They all have texture. As a matter of fact, even vanilla ice cream has texture, but for some reason the word, texture, has now come to mean only rough or bumpy. Usually if a fabric is spoken of as *textured*, it's because the quality is poor, and the dye didn't come out right, and they can't think of anything else to say about it.

Now that you know all you need to know about furniture design and fabrics, we will consider the articles of furniture you will require. Furniture can be divided into four simple but thought-provoking categories. Things to sit on (such as beds, chairs, ottomans, benches, settees, love seats), things to lie down on (such as beds, cots, *chaises longues*—dig that French spelling—sofas, couches, davenports), things to put things on (such as beds, dining tables, end tables, night tables, coffee tables, tea tables, whatnots, *étagères*, *étuis*, *épergnes*, *estaminets*, and esprit de corps), and things to put things in (such as chests*, highboys, lowboys, bureaus, cabinets, breakfronts, hutch tables—so called because they were once used to keep the rabbits in in the the winter—firkins, coffee cans, sewing baskets, old shoe boxes, attic stairs, etc.). There are some articles for which no furniture has yet

*Bet you thought I was going to say beds again.

been designed, and you will discover these for yourself if you look around your house at the objects
which have collected on tops of bookcases, in stair
wells, and closet floors. This is an opportunity for
some unknown talented designer. There is a crying
need for a graceful and beautifully proportioned arti-
cle of furniture in which to keep one galosh, a dented
trumpet, a movie film splicer and a stilt needing repairs. Furniture is in its infancy.

Besides furniture, there are other necessary furnishings which are all part of interior decoration, and
the most important is floor coverings. There are many
types of floor coverings and what you select depends
to a large extent on just how good an education you
had planned for the children. If they wanted to go

to medical school, for instance, you might have the whole house carpeted wall-to-wall.

If you were only going to send them through high school, linoleum rugs are for you. In between linoleum rugs and carpets there are many types of floor tiles and rugs, but you mustn't forget to integrate them with the shelf edging in the linen closet.

There are many kinds of fine carpet, like Axminster, Velvet, Wilton, Stilton, and Munster. Rugs can be cotton or wool, domestic or imported, Turkish, Chinese, Persian, Indian, smooth, shaggy or threadbare. Most rugs are expensive, and besides they're terribly technical, with number of threads to the inch, methods of knotting, and so forth. I don't know that I'd buy rugs or carpets at all, if I were you. Why don't you paint the floor? That would be a *fun* project for the whole family, and the children could help spatter.

If you do decide on rugs, it is important that you buy rug cushions to fit, as this will keep the rugs from skidding and will also prolong their life. It also makes an *extra layer* for the children to sweep broken crayons into, where they will be entirely unnoticed until the first time you send the rug to be cleaned. This is also true of Turkish taffy, banana flavor. However, the chief importance of the rug cushion is that sooner or later it peeps out from beneath the rug, and gives the entire house a certain air of *sans-souci*. This is an excellent way to show the world that *you* care more for your family than for mere possessions and that you are a better mother than Mrs. Johnson down the street whose rugs are never askew but whose children, you can bruit it about, are *starved* for affection.

After floors are covered, the next most important thing to be covered is windows. In the old days, women used to hang curtains at windows. First the windows were put in the houses so people inside could see out. Then housewives put curtains in front of them so people outside couldn't see *in*. But nowadays, *nobody* hangs curtains. They *treat windows*. You don't go to a store and say, "What kind of curtains shall I buy?" You go in and say, "I'd like some advice on how best to treat my windows, which present a problem." *All* windows present a problem, and if you forget it you will lose caste instantly and be fobbed off on some tyro in the kitchen-curtain department who doesn't know beans about window treatments. How you treat your window depends on whether you're trying to make them look bigger or smaller or wider, or hide them altogether, or pretend one is there that isn't, or tie them in with a bookcase, or treat three windows as one, or maybe even just leave them bare. The last suggestion is probably altogether too radical, though, so unless you're on terribly good terms with your neighbors, and always lend them the leaf sweeper or the four eggs, I wouldn't try it. We do it, but we can get away with it because we once had someone visit us in a white Jaguar and it raised the tone of the neighborhood so much that we don't even have to rake up our leaves any more.

(Actually, the owner of the Jaguar had lost his way, and came in to ask if he might use the telephone to call his friend and get directions for finding his way out of the slum he'd got lost in. But the neighbors don't know *that*.)

We will explain the different types of window treatment quickly, so take a deep breath. There are plain old window shades on rollers that you pull up and down with a string, or a crocheted loop, or a plastic parrot, or a phosphorescent knob, or something. Sometimes they snap up by themselves and frighten everybody, and they're no longer considered terribly chic by the elite. Then there are fancy shades, with stripes or flowers and scallops and fringe. But you have to be wary with those. Look out for the wallpaper, they're going to clash! Next there is the plain old-fashioned glass curtain, so called because it isn't made of glass at all. (If it were, it would be called Fiberglas.) Glass curtains are just plain old curtains that hang on a plain old curtain rod and are made of net, or nylon, or silk gauze, or ninon and you can see through them. (Maybe *that's* why they're called glass curtains.) Then there's the kind that's ruffled and tied back, or criss-crossed, very frothy and pretty, very ironing and starching. They're very good for showing off what a good housekeeper you are, never mind what Mrs. Johnson says. Next, there are draperies, which hang over the shades or glass curtains, and can either just hang at the sides of the windows, or can be on a pulley and be drawn across the windows at night. They take a great deal of material, usually expensive, plus a great deal of lining, also a great deal of careful tailoring, and when you're all through, the traverse rod gets stuck. Oh well. Then consider the overdrape. This goes over the drapery, and is so formal that you cannot call anyone by his first name in that room. And I'm beginning to feel as though I'm wearing hoopskirts and whalebone and I'd better get on to the next thing because it's hard to breathe. If all this isn't enough, there is the valance, the cornice and even the swag. These cover the *tops* of the curtains, draperies, overdrapes, shades, blinds and so on, which is terribly neat but leave the bottoms hanging out, which is terribly untidy. Please don't ask me why. Now I'm all worn out, and we've hardly mentioned Venetian blinds yet, and they're terribly hard to dust. So we'll just skip the whole thing. It's all very exhausting, because we almost forgot that not only do you have to keep all this clean, you have to wash the windows too. So why don't *you* have a friend stop by with a Jaguar? Or better still, have the dealer drop one off for you to try. You don't *have* to buy it.

Accessories are an important part of a charmingly decorated home as they accent the general design of the room by giving added interest in line, color, form or mass. They may complement the color scheme or provide a needed spot of sharp contrast. Sometimes they serve as conversation pieces. I don't know just what a conversation piece is for exactly, because if you and your guest can't think of anything to say to each other but "My, what an interesting ashtray," it's my opinion you shouldn't have invited the guest in the first place. Why didn't you invite a friend instead? Of course if the guest just dropped in without warning, that's another matter. In that case, instead of depending on the ashtray, it would be simpler to explain that you have two cases of chicken pox going on upstairs. Ashtrays are shaky foundations for an evening's conversation—I don't care if they *were* part of a Locomobile hubcap.

Accessories include lamps, knick-knacks, bric-a-brack, objets d'art, gimcracks, gew-gaws, orange satin pillows that say "Souvenir of Pinkertown" or "I Pine For You And Balsam" and all the carefully selected exquisite little things that express your personality and taste.

Lamps, of course, are intensely necessary if you are to find your way about after dark, and there are several kinds. There are lamps that were once coffee mills, oil lamps, old sewing machine pedals, wine coolers, apothecaries' jars, kitchen pumps, candle stands and all the other common ordinary types. But of course lamps that were once hitching posts, umbrella stands or slop basins are far better. And the really *good* ones are made from such unlikely beginnings that you have to ask, "What *is* it." Coal hods, fire buckets, shoe trees—all excellent. And if you can think up a way to turn an old curling iron into a dainty little vanity table lamp, you are *made*.

Some women like to display collections of old glass or china, pewter, silver, shells, etc., arranged beautifully and proudly in elegant polished cabinets. A collection finishes off a room attractively, and displays far more than the mere objects. It displays your interest in your home, your own personality, your hobby, and can be a focal point for the whole room. There are endless fascinating things to be collected, and you can get your friends to help you. I collect Cellini bowls, myself, but I haven't gotten too far with it yet. The antique shops in my neighborhood have very depleted stocks. In the meantime, just to amuse myself, I collect money.

If you find, as you complete your home, that the little finishing details are getting too expensive, and your husband is getting too insistent about needing an overcoat, there *are* other ways to acquire them. We have acquired two Goya etchings, several North American wrought-iron insects, a copy of a carved Egyptian owl from the Louvre, a Toulouse-Lautrec lithograph, a Daumier, a beautiful Japanese water-color of a cat, two ancient Roman oil lamps dug up in Eritrea, a pair of silver hurricane lamps, a pre-Columbian Aztec idol, and a lovely white Limoges coffee set, all by the simple expedient of admiring them in other people's houses until they took the hint. Some of them were not exactly given to us. They were more or less sort of, well, stolen. A few were actually given to us because the owners were somehow led to believe that my husband was going to repair them and return them. He did repair them, of course. We just haven't returned them yet. With a little practice and an honest open face, you too can have lovely things for *your* home.

Now we are ready to start the step-by-step actual decorating of your home, and the very first thing is to decide on your color scheme. Now is the time to fling off the yoke of convention, and let yourself go. There is no color scheme that isn't right if you like it. It would be too bad to finish the whole job and then find that it was really very ordinary, so don't be afraid to take chances. What you want is something different, something that will make your friends talk. Try doing a room in black and purple, with perhaps a puce accent just for laughs. Then invite your friends in for an evening of Russian roulette.

Remember that color, and color alone, will give your home its individual character, and an exciting choice of colors that suit your own personality can give your living room an air of distinguished sophistication and good taste that will endure even after it's all dingy and shabby again, which will be soon. Very soon. Probably, with a little extra effort on the part of stray children, cats and other extraneous matter that drift into your home, day after tomorrow.

If you follow accurately the following few simple rules, you should have really striking results. So pay close attention, follow the easy steps, and go ahead with confidence:

I. Choose your favorite color and then immediately eliminate that as a possibility. If you go spreading your favorite color all over your walls, you're going to get awfully sick of it. Choose one you're not really crazy about, and you'll find you're far less likely to tire of it. This is your *basic color*.

II. Now, for the proper accent, choose carefully a color that is much darker or much lighter than the first, and of a different hue and intensity. Should it happen, by some horrid mischance, that at any time you select Cream, Oatmeal, or Tan, discard them immediately as possibilities. The reason for this is extremely technical, and without professional training you probably wouldn't understand the reason which is that I can't stand the sight of them.

III. For the next two colors, to be used in small areas for that exhilarating touch of spice, you can safely let yourself go, even to the wildest flights of lime, avocado, or persimmon. Watermelon and raspberry are nice, too, if in season and thoroughly ripe.

This is now *your personal* color scheme selected by *you*, to suit your personality. Only you will have this highly individual color combination, chosen to enhance your complexion, hair-coloring and your favorite nail polish.

That is, if what you wanted was an *analogous* color scheme. Now if you prefer an *anachronous* color scheme, or even a *contiguous, homologous, monochromatic* or *monogamous* color scheme the whole subject becomes far more difficult and complex. For an anachronous color scheme, you simply turn the clock back. For a monochromatic, or homogenized color scheme, use plain white for everything, with a dash of oyster to give the eye something to stop at. However, for a monogamous color scheme, you'll have to get an interior decorator as this is not for the amateur.

You are now ready to go ahead and paint or paper your rooms. There are two generally accepted methods of doing this. One is to get out the ladders and buckets and brushes and take off a little weight (and you *have* been gaining a bit, right here. I couldn't help noticing) and the other is to call up a house painter and let *him* take off a little weight. Do not be fooled into thinking one is necessarily easier than the other. Each method has its disadvantage, or to put it bluntly, they're both horrible.

Let us start with the professional house painter. He has a mean nasty disposition, and he knows, from bitter experience, that all women are perfect idiots who haven't the remotest idea what they want on their walls. But you surprise him. You know *exactly* what you want. The only trouble is that none of the samples he paints on the wall for you is *quite* it. After he has put enough samples on the wall for you to be sure he's really working hard enough, and just when his nerves are at the breaking point, tell him it's *almost* right, but just to add the least bit of umber. He will be so stunned by your amazing knowledge of pigments that he will then be your slave, and when you get to the dining room with that tricky shade of not quite ripe apricot, he won't mind in the least mixing up a new batch of paint for the seventeenth time. I absolutely guarantee this method of handling the contrary house painter. Without knowing this secret password, you are lost. He will have the upper hand, and he won't *let* you have white trim on the woodwork or a different color on the insides of the bookcases. He'll tell you about the houses he has painted in *much* better neighborhoods than yours, and he'll insist that nobody over in Apple Knolls *ever* has white trim. So *remember the touch of umber*.

Never forget that what goes on between you and the professional house painter is open warfare and you must be on the *qui vive* at every moment. From the day he starts, his object is to frustrate you in every possible way, and to lose all the really important screws from the bathroom fixtures so that you can never again have a towel rack. When he takes down the pictures, something happens to the hooks and wires. This is his secret weapon, to which your only defense is hiding his work clothes when he leaves for the day. His M.O. (I watch Dragnet too) is never never to finish one room at a time. Heavens! He'd be drummed out of the corps and stripped of his paper cap and drop cloths. He does a little bit to every room in the house to get started, and his next step (should the weather be mild and lovely) is firmly to glue down all the windows.

He is a character, and he will never let you forget it. Whatever color you have always wanted on the

inside of your own closet, that is the one color he won't let you have. He will stand in the doorway of the closet, his arms spread protectively across it, and his eyes will fill with tears. "I can't do it," he says. "You *won't like it*." You really will like it, but you'll never get a chance to find out. "Please take my advice," he pleads. "*I* know you won't be happy with it." Here he is telling the simple truth. Whatever the outcome, you won't be happy with it, because in this situation you cannot win. You have already expended all your energy in the struggle over the bedroom walls, and you are now too tired to fight. *He* knows you won't be happy with it. He met you only the day before yesterday, but *he* knows what color you will or won't be happy with. The touch of umber, so successful in the living room, will not work in the bedroom closet because he has now learned the counter-attack. He does not put any sample on at all until your defenses have crumbled and, sorrowful and beaten, you say, "Go ahead. Paint it tan. I'm sure it will be lovely. I would have hated deep blue." This is the one moment during the whole hideous affair when you will hear him whistle at his work.

Your alternative to the house painter is to do the job yourself, and in this case, the absolutely most important thing to remember is to CALL THE HOSPITAL and make the reservation first. This hint to successful painting and papering is not to be found in any other books on the subject.

There are many new types of paint on the market,

and of course your paint dealer is the person to consult about the special qualities and advantages of each. Many of them have a remarkable permanence as I can personally attest. Four years ago I used a new type of high-gloss enamel in my kitchen, and the resulting white streaks in my hair are still there.

Naturally before you start any painting you must first prepare your walls. They need a good scrubbing with a detergent made for that purpose, and here is where your husband comes in. On the other hand, if he's smart, here is where he goes out.

Now you are ready to mix your paints, but keep your wits about you and remain calm. Everything may yet turn out all right. What you are aiming for is a terribly subtle shade of gray with warm overtones and cool undertones and just a hint of green with the merest suggestion of blue. You start by opening a can of white paint. But it won't open. So you go down to the cellar for a good strong screw driver, and that breaks so you try the beer bottle opener. Maybe it would be best to wait till your husband comes home tonight and you can start mixing paints tomorrow. Of course he may not come home tonight. If he has any experience at all he very likely may not be home for several weeks. He was opposed to the whole idea anyway, if you remember. He didn't mind the house being shabby. He even *liked* it that way. However, if he should decide to risk it, perhaps he will open the can for you.

Tomorrow will come, inevitably, and there you

are with an opened can of white paint. Now go out and run around the yard and see if you can find a good stick for stirring. No? Well, try that screw driver again. That will be a dandy stirrer. Stir the paint well. This is absolutely and utterly vital. Let the children stir it for a while. Now run down to the hardware store and buy some of those paper buckets that are made for mixing paints (what *won't* they think of next!) and come back. Oh dear, the paint has all settled again.

Now start pouring the white paint back and forth from the paint can to the bucket. *Did* you buy the small buckets? That's a *shame*. Doesn't quite fit in, does it? A good deal splashed on the floor? Oh well, that's part of the *fun*. The baby crawled through it? The dog rolled in it? Too bad. Now is the time for aspirin. And maybe just a *touch* of vodka.

Now your white paint is thoroughly stirred and mixed. Add just the least little bit of black. Stir it well. Not quite enough black. Add a bit more. Stir again. Still not enough. Add just the least little drop more—stop!—that's enough. Now stir again. Still not enough? Oh well, throw in a big glob this time. Stir it up. Goodness! It's *much* too much, isn't it? It's *quite* too dark. And you can't add any more white because the bucket is now full. Well, pour some of it off into the paint can, and run down and buy some more buckets and some more white paint. Remember to get the bigger buckets this time, hey?

Now you have achieved the proper *tone* of gray,

[87]

but of course it's just plain old gray. Now for the subtlety. SUBTLE *OVERTONES* ARE ALWAYS GAINED BY THE ADDITION OF UMBER. Never forget this rule. SUBTLE *UNDERTONES* ARE ACHIEVED BY THE ADDITION OF SIENNA. Never forget this one either. They're really more for conversation than for practical use, but very effective. The suggestion of blue is got by adding the merest suggestion of blue, and the hint of green can best be accomplished by the delicate drop by drop addition of green with a *light hand*. Fold your ingredients in gently with a wooden spoon and taste often.

All in all, the main thing to remember in mixing paints is to buy enough of those little paper buckets.

And keep at it. If you don't get the right color today, maybe you will tomorrow. If all else fails, you can always choose another color. White might be chic at that.

The most fun in painting a room is the painting of the window mullions. This is done with a special brush called a sash tool and a very steady hand. If your hand is not steady, the rest of the work is done with a razor blade and of course here is where the smaller children can help. Give each child his own little pane of glass to clean, and his own little razor blade for scraping, and you could make a game of it and offer a prize for the best job. A little Band-Aid would be a good inexpensive prize.

When you are doing an entire room over, it is wisest to start with the ceiling and work your way down. An excellent trick to remember, to help you in painting ceilings, is to cut a rubber ball in half, and put the handle of the brush through it so that it acts as a cup to catch the drips. Then when you bring your hand down to load the brush again, you get a whole cupful of paint at once on your upturned face, instead of continual drips. If the ceiling is all that needs doing, it is still wisest to start with the ceiling and work your way down, as it is not possible just to paint a ceiling.

As a matter of fact, it is not possible just to paint any part of a house at all. You might just as well start with a corner of the attic ceiling and keep going till you work your way out the cellar door, because you never will find a good stopping place till you're outside the house. You may not even find a good stopping place *there*. I once started out to paint a clay flower pot white and ended up doing not only the house, but the garage, a fence and three outdoor chairs, and had to be forcibly restrained from starting on the neighbors' garages which then looked awfully dirty next to ours. So remember to *BUY PLENTY OF PAINT*.

The hazards of painting are, of course, drips, spots, the painting of things you hadn't meant to paint, the failure to paint things you had meant to paint, and the awful danger of paint on pets. Paint on pets is a difficult problem, and one to which, so far as I know, there is no solution. Cats and birds may attempt to remove the paint themselves (birds going so far as to moult in an effort to remove it) but the results are often disappointing and the animal may become highly nervous and discouraged. Dogs ignore it, which is probably the most sensible approach after all. Paint *can* be removed from human beings to a large extent, and here time is your greatest ally.

DO NOT BE MISLED BY THE TOM SAWYER FABLE. Many people have started out to do a painting job under the misapprehension that neighbors, relatives, friends and delivery men will all come and lend a hand. They will not. Did you think you were the only one who read Tom Sawyer? They will very likely not come to the house at all until the job is finished, unless it's to ask you to lend them eight dollars and ninety-four cents to pay for a package that just came C.O.D. from Macy's. The only people who might offer their help are children under four, and my advice to you is to refuse it graciously.

If you have never tried wallpapering I can assure you that a good job can be done by the amateur, and it is perhaps the quickest way to effect a complete change in a room. The wallpaper store will sell you a kit containing all the necessary tools, and they will also be glad to help you figure out how many rolls you will need. You will have to provide yourself with a ladder, and a very large table.

The paste is mixed to the consistency of sticky cream and is spread carefully and smoothly on the paper. It is preferable to spread it on the back of the paper. You then simply stick the paper on the wall. You'd be surprised how often it really sticks, too.

You start in a corner of the room, hoping for the best, and you keep going till you get around to the beginning again. DON'T GO OUT THE DOOR, or you'll find yourself papering the whole hall and that's the wrong paper for there.

In wallpapering, it is important to try not to get the pattern upside down as this may later prove to be very disturbing, and it will be very hard to match the last strip to the first one. The whole object of course is to *try* to match the pattern at the edges.

It is also a good idea to hang the strips up and down. If they should also chance to be vertical it is all to the good as if they are too much off plumb, you

will always have to stand at an angle in that room which you might get accustomed to, but which might be very disconcerting to guests. Some old houses are all out of plumb to begin with. Some new houses are too. This presents a problem in papering. The question is, should you hang the paper straight, and let the doors and windows and floors appear crooked, or should you hang the paper crooked too? In this situation your best choice would be to take all the paper back to the store while you can still get your refund. Or, again, you might keep the paper and buy a better house.

Many other problems arise in papering which it would be well to discuss here. These problems are wrinkling, slipping, tearing and failure to adhere. There are also outside corners and inside corners. Now that we have discussed these problems, you can go ahead and repaper your living room.

Oh, have you finished? Too bad. Because I forgot to tell you one thing. Before putting up the new paper, it is absolutely advisable to remove every trace of the old paper first, and it is also advisable to take down most of the pictures before you start or the new paper will not lie *smooth*.

Well, better luck next time.

After all the painting and papering is done, everything else is easy. It is simply a matter of shopping, and purchasing what you need, which is a good pair of arch supports and a footbath. For it is only now, with the walls all nicely papered or painted in that perfectly divine shade of off-mustard, that you find that off-mustard is just not *it* this year, and not one manufacturer has made one yard of off-mustard fabric of any kind. You cannot even get a yard of off-mustard fringe or gimp or galloon either. So pick a new color and start over.

Once you have selected your carpets or rugs, and you have ordered all the furniture and draperies, you have only to sit back comfortably on your bare floor and wait. You wait and wait and wait. You call up. You argue. You cajole. You threaten. But it is no use. There is no password for upholsterers as there is for painters. Upholsterers cannot be hurried. Christmas comes and goes, Easter is approaching. And at last the great day comes. The sofa is being delivered. You wait trembling at the door while the men take it off the truck. They bring it into the room. It's beautiful! It's everything you ever hoped for. It's big and comfortable and terribly smart, and it exactly fits the space between the windows where you had intended it to go. There is only one thing wrong. They have put the wrong fabric on it.

A well-known psychoanalyst, Dr. Milton R. Sapirstein, in his book *Paradoxes of Everyday Life* has written about women and the interior decoration of their homes and says that this is a time of major crisis, similar to childbirth, marriage and the death of a loved relative. During the period of decoration, he says, a woman who is not utterly well-balanced is

likely to find the whole thing beyond her emotional capacity, and end up in a sanitarium. I know of a woman who entered a six-year period of indecision because of her continual confrontation with a lamp finial out of character in an otherwise perfectly decorated room. Now I do not believe that need unduly frighten you. It is exactly to *prevent* this sad outcome that I have prepared this work. It is my belief that if you have carefully read this chapter, and followed my simple instructions, you can accomplish the whole job without a nervous collapse. A little *crise de nerfs*, perhaps, a few weeks rest at home in a darkened room with a good nurse and plenty of phenobarbital, and you'll be almost as good as new. And as soon as *you've* recovered, you can start fighting with that man who upholstered the sofa and see if you can get *him* to recover. Or maybe it would be quicker and simpler in the long run just to paint the whole room over.

EIGHT

Simple Home Repairs
That Even You Can Do

You can easily, with a few simple tools, attend to most of the decay and dilapidation of your own home. These constant despairs come under the headings of PLUMBING, WIRING, SCREAMING AT APPLIANCES, also a bit of MOTH PREVENTION and the even more important PREVENTION OF MOTH PREVENTION which is far more time-saving and absolutely perfect housekeeping than any of the others, even.

We will take each of these up in order, and then gently put them down again.

The first subject to be discussed is PLUMBING. In case you have ever wanted to categorize plumbing, allow me to suggest that it goes right in there with death and taxes, and the only reason Ben Franklin forgot it is because he didn't have any as it hadn't been invented yet, bless it. The main thing to remember here is that PLUMBING IS FUN! It also promises to be the messiest part of the whole book, because, whether you like it or not, your house is *full* of plumbing. There are pipes all over the place, in the walls and in the cellar, carrying water upstairs and down, hot and cold, dirty and clean. These pipes are vital. They are also rusty, full of sediment, and READY TO LEAK AT ANY MOMENT! (Look out! Do you hear something dripping?) The rule to remember in plumbing is: SOMETHING SOMEWHERE IS LEAKING. Often you can hear the leak for some time before you can actually see the stain on the new wallpaper.

Not all leaks are confined to the house, however. Often a good one can develop in the pipes leading into your house, under your front lawn. These leaks may go unnoticed for quite a while while your lawn gets curiously greener and greener and your water bill gets curiously bigger and bigger. Don't waste time calling the water department, for the leak is *just* this side of your property line. What you do is call in someone to start digging. And just when the lawn was doing so nicely, too.

Of course not all leaks result from faulty plumbing. Some leaks are due to rain coming in through roofing and siding and flashing, some are due to children practicing their Australian crawl in the bath-

tub, and some are due to Dacron shirts hung too en-
thusiastically dripping. (Say, look at that funny stain
on the living-room ceiling. Was that there before?)

The equipment you need for plumbing is: 1. An
enameled pail; 2. a dry wet mop (do not attempt to
substitute a wet dry mop); and 3. the phone number
of a good plumber.

If you want to do a really professional job, you
also want to supply yourself with a flashlight, a set
of wrenches, some washers, a hammer, and a pair of
India rubber boots. The flashlight is what you use
for peering under sinks and behind washing machines
and sometimes is used to find your way to the cellar
during Electrical Repairs which we will discuss later
after we get through with all this awful mess. The
hammer is for hitting on pipes in the cellar. From upstairs this will sound as though something wonderful
is being accomplished, whereas in actual fact all that
is being accomplished is that a new leak has now ap-
peared in the stricken pipe. The wrenches should be
carried around with you in a little black leatherette
case, and you could, if you wished, try wrenching
something with them. It makes a very good impres-
sion, though needless to say, goodness knows what
might happen. A good thing to do before starting any
plumbing whatever is to turn off all the water. There
are valves all over the cellar and if you try enough,
one of them is bound to be it.

After you have made a lot of noise, it is time to call
the plumber. Always keep in mind that it costs more

to have the plumber than the doctor. I don't know what you can do about it, but keep it in mind anyway. It will come in handy sometime to add to your list of grievances when you're in a complaining mood.

Electrical work is accomplished quite simply by the amateur, and you'll be amazed at what you can do, provided you remember NEVER TO STAND IN A POCL OF WATER WHILE YOU'RE DO- ING IT as wet feet can often bring on a cold, with the ever-present possibility of pneumonia, and com- plications. The most important electrical work is done in the cellar and is called CHANGING A FUSE, and this is most often necessary after attempting other types of electrical work. The fuse is a small frighten- ing glass object which blows out and has to be re- placed. It is found in a little thing with a door on it, and there are sometimes quite a lot of fuses.* The first step is to decide which is the blown-out fuse, and I can't tell you how to do that as I haven't yet found out how myself. But it doesn't matter as you can just try them all till you find the one that makes the lights go back on again, or the iron heat up again, or the washing machine start again. The next step, and this is the one really tricky bit, is to find the little box of new fuses. It could be on top of that old cup- board in the cellar where you keep paints and turpen- tine and stuff, but it isn't, is it? It *could* be on that little

---

*Once in a while a fuse is cunningly hidden *inside* a machine or appliance. This is very underhanded of the manufacturers and is done purely out of spite.

ledge on the cellar stairs, but—no—it isn't. It *might* be on the work bench where your husband always meant to make you that little extra shelf for the dining room for those pretty fruit plates. No. It's not there either. *Could* it be on the shelf where you keep the laundry soaps and bleaches? No. Maybe it's in that big box in the corner of the cellar where you keep old violin strings and broken lamp bases and lost car ashtrays? Nope. Not there. Well, dammit, how are you going to do your electrical repairs when everybody is so absolutely uncooperative? Wait! Maybe it's on that top shelf out in the pantry behind the box of used-up flashlight batteries under the ice cube tray with the broken lever. Yes! It is! Goody! Now take it down to the fuse box, unscrew the blown fuse, and carefully put in the new one. I wonder if it matters that the old one says 15W and the new one says 50W? Oh, well. There goes the washing machine again, and yes, the children are shouting down that the lights are on again, and you have done it! And if you don't turn on too many things at once, there's even a chance that you may not have a fire after all. A word of caution: In all electrical repairing, it is vital to remember to pay your fire-insurance premiums.

The next kind of electrical work that you can do is just as simple. Suppose you find that your house is really inadequately wired, and you don't have nearly enough outlets. You buy any number of multiple outlets and extension cords. You plug the multiple outlets in where you need the more wiring and then you plug in all the extension cords. Now you can have lamps, radio, television, a heater perhaps, or an air conditioner, and even an iron all going at once in the same room. Isn't that grand? Now you go back to step one, changing the fuse.

Screaming at appliances is something that is bound to go on practically all the time as appliances are bound to break down and always need cleaning anyway, and the service man charges $5.50 just to come to the back door, ring the bell, and say, "Good morning." So roll up your sleeves and let's clean the washing machine! You should do this at least twice a year, and much *much* oftener if you wash very lint-making things in it, such as clothing, towels, etc. First yank off the whole top of the machine. No, on second thought, first unplug the machine. Then yank off the top. Should you have the type of washer that opens in the front, yank off the whole front—I *guess*. Well, yank off something. Heavens, you can't expect me to know *everything*. Now that you have the whole top off, or the front off, or something, unscrew the top of that thing in the middle, and lift it out. Now remove that thing in the middle, and lift it out. Now remove that funny shaped thing with the holes in it, and lift that out. Now take out the whole activator. If you haven't got an activator, take out the agitator. If you haven't got an agitator, take out the tumbler. If you haven't got a tumbler I don't know what you should do. I've got enough to do without answering so many questions. Now. Remove the wash basket. Look out! Heavy, wasn't it. Hurt your foot much? Now remove that sort of queer-shaped thing at the side, and you should now be looking into a great big thing with lima bean shaped holes in the bottom. Now reach down into those holes and—ugh! Isn't it awful? Sort of wet and gooey. Oh, *there's* that other brown sock. Too bad you've already thrown away the mate because you'd given this one up for lost. Now just clean up the machine nicely, and put it all back together again. If there are any pieces left over, put them in that box with the violin strings. They may come in handy some time for fixing the washing machine. Take all the lint that you have scraped out of the machine and put it into a receptacle

of some sort (a wheelbarrow will do nicely) and drag it outside to the trash can where the sanitation men will take it on their truck and so on and so on.

The refrigerator requires intense and desperate cleaning all the time. Every minute of the day and night things are spilling in it, frost is building up in it, and things are getting lost on the backs of the shelves and the mold is growing tall on them. Seedless grapes are rolling under the hydrators and cake frosting is glueing itself onto all those wire racks. So don't waste a minute. Remove everything from the refrigerator but the enamel and the manufacturer's name in chromium letters and you will find all kinds of goodies you never suspected you had. And you've had them for years, too. Take all of these interesting goodies gingerly and dump them in the garbage pail. Resolve never *never* to let the refrigerator go without cleaning again for more than three days. (You needn't actually *do* it, of course. Just *resolve* to do it. Nobody will ever notice those little grapes down there, and in time they'll disintegrate most likely. Of course when the refrigerator gets so full of half-eaten cans of peaches and little bowls of left-over string beans that the door won't close, you'll probably feel that you want to get after it a bit.)

Moth prevention is an important job and it is not likely that anyone else in the family will do it for you. If it is not done, moths will come and lay their little eggs in all the winter coats and sweaters and blankets and then the little babies will hatch out and eat all the winter coats and sweaters and blankets. This is very good nutrition for the moths, and remember that it is *their way of life*. They don't come and stop you from eating steak, do they? That is our way of life. So it is obvious that what you want is the prevention of moth prevention—which is only fair—and far more relaxing than moth prevention. The method of prevention of moth prevention is actually a double blessing as it is good for you, good for the moths, good for business, good for closet cleaning and in fact the only people it isn't good for are the moth preventive manufacturers who can easily go into some other less horrible line of work. Besides benefiting all these people, prevention of moth prevention eliminates a great hazard to the housekeeper which comes of getting out a blanket and having moth crystals scatter all over the floor and under the beds and bureaus, requiring an enormous amount of sweeping up and the breathing in of noxious fumes.

Prevention of moth prevention is actually so labor-saving that you will be grateful to me for years and years to come and some civic-minded organization will probably make me an award of some kind for my spectacular work for the benefit of humanity. Think of it! Never again do you have to clean out all those musty closets and dusty bureau drawers and cart all those itchy woolen things around to attics. Never again do you have to struggle with defiant garment bags, belligerent blanket bags and tar paper and cleaning things and spraying things. Just leave every-

thing where it is, and sit down and read a book. Next fall when your husband shows you his winter overcoat with all the fuzz eaten off, you say, "Tsk, tsk. But I think black would be so *much* more becoming as long as you're getting a new one." He has really wanted a new overcoat for three years anyway, so he is actually delighted. Everyone is delighted. The children can get a new sweater and a new pair of mittens each, you can get a new fur coat (that old thing was really a disgrace) and you can get those new blankets you've been wanting. If you're clever, you can discover all this early, and get in on all those August sales, and save *lots* of money. They say seal is going to be very chic this year and you could get one of those darling fuzzy beige hats to go with it.

NINE

Gardening, Yet

I have now stalled off any mention of gardening about as long as I can because sooner or later this book is going to have to end, and like it or not, gardening *is* part of housekeeping. I wanted to give you the same absolutely perfect methods to use here as in the other phases of housekeeping. But truth will out. When it comes to gardening—well, to put it plainly —everything I touch *withers*. It's lucky I wasn't born till the twentieth century, or I'd have been sure Hawthorne had me in mind when he wrote "Rappacini's Daughter."

Around here, every time it rains too much, everyone says, "Well we really need the rain." Well *they* do. *They* have lawns and flowers and vegetables. We have a quarter of an acre of something hard and brownish. I hesitate to call it earth. I've often thought we ought to go into the pottery business instead of fighting those radishes year after year. This year I planted a few zinnias because it gets too embarrassing cutting our neighbors' zinnias year after year, and it's also too embarrassing to have friends come up from the city and have no flowers at all on the table. A neighbor told me you can't keep zinnias from coming up, but she doesn't know me. I did.

Once I put in some chrysanthemum plants, some daisies, some tulips and daffodils and crocuses, and then I sat back and said, "There!" But then the house painters came. Lots of them. And when they left we had a nice new coat of white paint on the house and beautiful glossy black shutters, and that same old quarter of an acre of something brown again. So I put in some more tulips and daffodils and crocuses and irises. I spent days on my hands and knees with a dibble.

We used to do all our work outside. I hesitate to call it gardening. But last year we got temporarily rich and my husband said he was too tired to mow any more, so we decided to have a Gardener. Well, he's not a Gardener, exactly. He comes with a truck and criticizes. He also has several brothers. They're thrown in. Mike—that's the Gardener's name—throws in lots of things. He rings the back door bell, and when I come, he says, "Mrs. Smith, I just wanted to tell you—I put in some snapdragons for you."

"But, Mike," I protest, "I told you I *hated* snapdragons."

[107]

"Oh, that's all right," he says. "I won't charge for them. They'll come up nice. You'll like them."

We used to have a—well, as a matter of fact, it started when we bought the house and there was a moribund barberry hedge across the front of the lawn. (I use the word lawn carelessly.) That barberry was so pitiable that we decided to put it out of its misery, and my husband spent three days and the skin of both his hands getting it out. It was a sick hedge, but it had the *healthiest* roots. After he got it out, we regretted it instantly, because there was then an enormous bare brown ditch across the front of our property and it looked even worse than the sick hedge, and we couldn't even make crab grass grow there. Finally in despair we went to a nursery to see what we could get in the way of shrubs. Without money, that is. Well, that nursery man was very mercenary and he wouldn't give us any shrubs at all, so we finally made a swap. We gave him forty dollars and he gave us all the evergreens that had something wrong with them. They weren't sick or anything, just peculiar looking, lop-sided or stunted or funny shapes.

After we put them in the bare ditch, it didn't look too good, so we bought a hundred pachysandra plants and spent most of a week on our hands and knees, putting them around the evergreens, and after that— well, it didn't look much better. There was an awful lot of bare dirt between the plants. However, every- one assured us that it would spread rapidly and soon

we would have a lovely thick growth that would cover all the bare spots. And would you believe it? At the end of two years those pachysandra plants didn't cover a thing? Not even the wrapper from a piece of bubble gum with a picture of Rabbit Maranville on it.

So when we got rich and we got this Gardener, Mike, he said, "Mr. Smith, don't you think it would be nicer to move those shrubs back to the house to replace that overgrown forsythia that looks so ragged?" And Mr. Smith said yes, he did. So they took the only thing that has ever grown around here and threw it out. The forsythia was the one thing that enabled me to keep my head up. Every spring I could say, "Well, the forsythia is out," or "Well, spring is late this year; my forsythia isn't out yet."

It was *dependable*. So they yanked out all my forsythia, and moved the evergreens back to be the foundation planting. And in the moving all my tulips and daffodils and crocuses and irises got dug up and lost *again*.

Now our house is one of those big old-fashioned ones that they don't build them like that any more. Why should they? Who wants them? It's nice, though, you know? Comfortable, roomy, homey, warm, cozy, shabby, hard to clean. Anyway, it has a stone foundation, and the first floor is about six feet above the ground in the front, maybe ten feet at the back because of the slope of the ground. So you can't just put in a few little plants the way you can around a new house with maybe only two feet of basement showing. We need *plants*. There was this big tall thing planted in the front. Nobody knew what it was, but it was more of a tree than a shrub, and it had beautiful white blossoms on it every spring. (I couldn't nonchalantly mention it when I talked about the forsythia, though—I didn't know its name.) It was *lovely*. It went right up to the second floor. I was proud of that tree.

So Mike (he's the Gardener, you remember) and his brother, they were standing out there admiring their work after they moved all the little lop-sided evergreens to the foundation, and presently they rang the door bell.

"Mrs. Smith,' Mike said. "I've been thinking. That tall bush, the one with the white flowers?"

"Yes," I said, starting to bristle.

"It's much too tall," Mike said. "Now that we've taken out all that great big ugly overgrown forsythia, and put in those small shrubs, that big thing is much too high for them. We thought we'd move it around to the back."

Well, in a way I thought he was right. There was no planting at all in the back, except for some watermelon seeds my youngest son had planted that hadn't grown.

"So," Mike said, when they'd moved it around to the back where it promptly died, "now there's that big empty space there in the front. Don't you think we ought to put in a rhododendron? Rhododendrons are pretty."

"Mike," I said, "I hate rhododendrons. I don't know why, but I simply cannot stand rhododendrons."

"Well," said Mike, "I just happen to have a nice rhododendron I could let you have cheap."

"Well," said I, "I don't care *what* they cost, I don't like the way they look."

"Well," said Mike, "I could let you have it for ten dollars. I'll just bring it around tomorrow, and you don't have to take it if you don't like it."

"I won't like it," I said, without much hope. He wasn't fooling me one bit. I knew how he happened to have a nice rhododendron. He just happened to have a nice rhododendron for me the same way he was going to have some nice forsythia for the person

[111]

whose rhododendron he had just pulled out because it was too big.

Meanwhile he had cut down a long row of forsythia that had been overgrowing itself along the driveway. "You don't want all that overgrown forsythia," Mike had said. "I'll just cut it back." I did want all that overgrown forsythia, but I was saving my strength. So he had cut it all down mercilessly, to about one inch, and I'm waiting for that to come back along with the dead tree without the white blossoms in the back yard. However, there, amid the shorn forsythia, standing all by itself and looking embarrassed was one tall evergreen.

"Look," I said, "how about moving that evergreen to this bare corner to replace the tree you put in the back yard, instead of the rhododendron I don't want."

Mike and his brother looked at the evergreen, and laughed uproariously. They slapped their thighs, and they nudged each other with their elbows, and each time they nudged, they burst into fresh peals of hilarity.

"That?" they said, laughing so hard that they doubled up. "That? Why you can't move a tree like that. A big tree like that? Why that tree has roots that go right under that stone wall there."

"Oh well," I said. "I just thought. It's just the right size, and it certainly doesn't look very nice where it is."

"Ha ha," they said. "Well, we're going home now, Mrs. Smith. We'll just bring that rhododendron along tomorrow."

I talked to my husband about it that night. "Bob," I said, "you've got to do something. Mike and his brother are bringing a rhododendron tomorrow and they're going to plant it in that bare spot in the front."

"Well tell them not to," he said. "I hate rhododendrons."

The next day when Mike arrived with his rhododendron (or rather with what I imagine is Mrs. Wallace-around-the-corner's rhododendron) my husband went outside to talk to him. He came back in about two minutes.

"That's all taken care of," he said cheerfully. "I just told him that we weren't crazy about rhododendrons and Mike's brother had a marvelous idea. They're going to move that tall evergreen from the driveway over in front of the house. They said it was just the right size anyway, and it looks sort of funny where it is."

When the job was done, Mike rang the doorbell. "I just want you to see how good it looks, Mrs. Smith," he said.

I went and looked.

"Did you have much trouble moving it?" I asked.

"Naw," he said, "a little tree like that?"

Every year, come August, I'm fighting off my friends and relatives and neighbors who come with bushel baskets of home-grown tomatoes. Even after you tell them you don't want them, they bring them anyway. *They* don't know what to do with them. My husband likes tomatoes, but the children don't and I don't, so last year when the Gardener suggested tomato plants, I said with caution, "Well, only one or two, Mike. We don't use many tomatoes."

"Well," he said, "what did you intend putting in?"

"I don't know," I said. "We never have much luck with anything. Every year I've tried, but in the spring we always have measles or mumps or mostly chicken pox, so I can never get out there just when it needs the most care."

The next day Mike came, and I saw him busily working out back, but I was trying to straighten out seven layers of a seven-layer cake at the moment so I didn't pay much attention. When he was through he rang the doorbell.

"Well," he said beaming, "I put in those tomato plants for you. And don't worry. You don't have to pay me for them now. I won't charge you for them unless they grow. I only put in two dozen, like you said."

"Two *dozen*," I said, recoiling in horror. "I meant *two*."

"Oh," he said. "Don't worry. You'll *like* them."

Well we liked them all right. We loved them lavishly. We cared for them, and we watered them, and we weeded them, and we worried about them, and in August the neighbors started bringing us theirs, and ours weren't out yet. Late in September we were thrilled to see little green buds, and by the end of October each plant had about four little hard

green tomatoes on it, the size of, oh, a marble maybe. We got them in just before the frost. They were sort of pretty to look at though.

After we lost all our chrysanthemums and daisies to the house painters and after we lost all our bulbs to Mike and his brothers, Mike came to me one day this spring, and said, "Mrs. Smith, have you thought about flowers?"

It was in the height of the chicken pox season so I hadn't thought much about flowers. But I said I had. I didn't want the Gardener to think I didn't care. "What I really want to do," I said, "is to get in some perennials again."

"How about petunias?" Mike said.

"Oh, no," I said. "I don't like petunias."

"How about some nice gladiolas?" he said.

"Oh no," I said. "I don't like gladiolas."

So the petunias and gladiolas are in. And I'll get to love them. Mike says so.

Actually, what has happened here, as you may already have figured out, is that in this case it is Mike who is the absolutely perfect gardener, and I have had to retire, my head bowed in shame, from the field of action. Or rather from the back yard.

So don't come to me with your gardening problems. If you want to be an absolutely perfect gardener you'll just have to do it on your own. Or maybe you should ask Mike.

TEN

Triumph Over Beds

A great many people have beds with accompanying bedding. Some housewives pull them apart every morning and then put them back together again. I think this is a nice attitude myself. However, the shocking truth is that there are some otherwise clean, healthy American women who do not make the beds absolutely every day. No one has ever dared to bring this fact out into the open before. They air the beds, but refuse to air the truth. Until now, this condition, though rife in some areas,* has been considered too appalling for public mention, but until it is faced fearlessly it cannot be effectively stamped out. A thing like this must be ruthlessly hunted and shot down before it spreads and infests larger and larger areas,

*As a matter of fact, this condition is rifest upstairs in the children's rooms. It's even pretty rife in our own room.

and we become a nation of sloths, all sleeping in unmade beds and smoothing out the wrinkles with our feet.

Even if you are the one in seven who makes the beds every day, it is important to know the proper method for making a bed. You are probably doing it very inefficiently, and thereby helping to give bed-making a bad name. Those who are guilty of not making the beds probably do so under the misapprehension that bed-making is necessarily difficult and time-consuming. Nothing could be further from the truth. Absolutely perfect bed-making is quick, simple and efficient. Once you acquire the proper habits there will no longer be any need for the slovenly conditions found in so many beds today.

The first step in proper bed-making is to strip the bed completely and air out the room. This is easily done by opening a window, or, if it should be too cold outside, blowing a few times. Next the mattress is turned. This is correctly done by grasping the mattress firmly at the side by the loops provided and flipping it lightly over. If, as you do this, you hear something

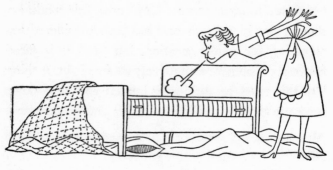

snap and find that you can't straighten up again, you haven't got the knack. Keep practicing. As soon as the mattress is turned, get out a file and smooth off your broken nails before going on to the next step. You don't want to snag the sheets, do you? You may also, if you wish, apply some liniment to your right shoulder.*

The next step is to put on the mattress pad or mattress cover, and this should be done now as it will be very hard to do it later.

The bottom sheet is put on next. This is important. If you mix up the sheets and accidently put the top sheet on the bottom and the bottom sheet on top, no one will get any sleep at all that night since they will all be suffering from vertigo. The bottom sheet must not only be put on the bottom, but also it is urgent that it be put on upside down and inside out to insure even wear. You see, the top sheet, which is *always* put on top (this is an absolute *rule*) is put on right side out and upside up. Then, when the sheets are changed, and the top sheet is put on the bottom (this is an exception to the rule above) it is then put on inside out and upside down and the new sheet is put right side out and upside up. You must understand however, that right side out for a top sheet is actually inside out, while inside out on the bottom sheet really means right side out. The reason for this is obvious—when you turn the top of the top sheet

*You may by now find it necessary to apply liniment to the mattress, too.

[119]

down, you want the turned-down part to be right side out, not inside out. (However, don't ever turn the bottom of the bottom sheet up as this would result in utter confusion.) If this is not clear, the simplest thing to do is to change both sheets at once, or, better still, provide a nice clean pile of sweet-smelling hay or straw which can be thrown out from time to time and replaced as needed.

We are now going to place the bottom sheet on the mattress. Some women throw the sheet over the mattress any old way, and then walk around and around the bed, tugging the sheet this way and that and smoothing it out and pulling it up and down till all the life has gone out of it. This is highly imperfect bed-making. The proper way is as follows. Take up the sheet in the hands. Grasp the sheet by the selvage at the side. Make sure the top of the sheet is toward the bottom of the bed and that the sheet is inside out (that is of course actually right side up). Also be sure the sheet is more or less centrally located, length-wise. Now stand by the side of the bed, with your feet parallel and toes pointing straight ahead. Hold your back straight, head up, chin in, etc. Now, with one small flick of the wrists the sheet should place itself on the bed, straight, centered and smooth. If it didn't, you didn't get the flick right. Try again tomorrow. But above all, don't touch it again now. If you start tugging it about, you will never learn the right flick.

The bottom sheet must be tucked in all around before even considering the top sheet. Some women do the head and foot first and then the sides. This is inefficient. The correct way is to start at the nearest corner, *miter it firmly no matter how it struggles,* and continue once around the bed, tucking in the sides and mitering corners as you go. When you have reached the starting place, DON'T LOOK BACK.

The placing of the top sheet is exactly like the placing of the bottom sheet (except that it is now right side up, which means inside out, and with its top facing the head of the bed). The top sheet is tucked in only at the bottom. Isn't that lucky? Do not tuck it too far in, as you may then pull out the whole business, bottom sheet and all, when you withdraw your hands. If you tuck it *too* far in, you may be trapped there and never get your hands out at all. Keep your enthusiasm in check at all times.

You may now place the blankets on the bed, using the same flick of the wrist. This is a very tricky business, because it sometimes happens that at this exact moment the cat suddenly decides to take a nap on that very bed and lands in the middle just as the blankets are settling down nicely into place. In this case it is best to remain calm. Continue to make the bed *around* the animal. This may leave an unsightly bump in the center of the bed, but eventually she is certain to get hungry and will leave of her own accord. Should she fail to do this, *call a veterinarian at once* as a healthy animal is always hungry, and she may be coming down with some obscure type of cat ailment. On the other hand, she may not be suffering from cat enteritis at all, but is simply having a litter of kittens. If this is the case, your best bet is to sleep in a semicircular position so as not to disturb the kittens until they are six weeks old and strong enough to make their way to somebody else's bed.

Once the blankets are on, you may fold down the top of the top sheet nicely over the blankets, and then proceed to tuck in the sides and miter the bottom corners. Some authorities believe that a fold should be made at the bottom of the bed to allow room for feet. I don't go along with this theory at all. There is no necessity for people to sleep on their backs with their feet sticking straight up. It is conducive to snoring. They should learn to sleep on their sides, with their feet nice and flat or folded well up toward the middle of the bed where there is more room. Or, better still, they can sleep on their stomachs with their toes curled down over the end of the mattress. There's *plenty* of room for their feet if they lie in the proper positions.

Many women, after making up the bed, cover it

all up with a bedspread. In certain cases, this may well be the wisest maneuver. Do not forget to place the pillow (having first shaken it well) neatly at the head of the bed as placing it at the foot will only confuse things further.

During the period in which you are acquiring the flick of the wrist and using the proper self-control in regard to straightening and tugging, there may be a certain amount of complaining on the part of your family. Don't let them get away with this. Explain to them that you have made the beds in strict accord with the finest authorities (that's me) and that if the sheets are wrinkled it is no doubt due to *improper entering of the bed* on their part. If they're just going to climb in any old way, you can't be blamed for wrinkles.

In time you will acquire the knack of absolutely perfect bed-making. Or they will become accustomed to wrinkles. (Tell them to think of their bed as a little nest.) Either way.

ELEVEN

How to Choose a Husband

Logically this is the first step in absolutely perfect housekeeping, as it is evident that without the proper husband you cannot possibly achieve this delightful goal. Of course one's assumption is that the bride's mother will impart such vitally important information to her, but for reasons that are not clear to me many mothers give their daughters information on a great many interesting matters, such as which are the best blankets to buy, and what kind of pot is best for pot roast, yet *fail to tell them the really necessary facts*. For that reason I feel it essential to give the information here, even though many people believe it to be the duty solely of the mother. As happiness cannot result from a marriage where the husband was selected in blind ignorance, we will here outline the most important factors in this momentous choice.

The very first thing to ascertain, before you let any relationship with a prospective husband go too far, is whether or not he has had the chicken pox. Don't just take his word for this. Demand to see a scar, or a doctor's certificate. You cannot be too careful about this. Should he fail this first test, forget him. He is not the man for you. Even though he may never get chicken pox, there is always the possibility that he *may* and the uncertainty will break down your own health. You will never know from day to day whether this might not be it, and you will study him anxiously every morning for signs of fever, headache and little spots. Every summer when he has mosquito bites you will spend sleepless nights. Should children result from this unsuitable marriage, the agony will deepen. When the children get to school age, day after day you will await their first symptoms with the increasing fear that your husband will catch it from them. The joys of springtime are gone forever for you, for the spring will bring only worry. When the day finally does come and all the children get chicken pox and last of all your husband turns up one morning with fever and headache and little red spots starting, YOU'LL BE SORRY. You'll cry, but it will be too late.

After you have checked on his immunity to chicken pox, find out whether any of his male relatives are bald. Should baldness show up anywhere in his family background, seek a husband elsewhere. Not that there is anything wrong with baldness in itself. A bald head can be entirely lovable. Some bald heads are even lovabler than some hairy ones. But not in a husband. This situation is economically unsound. Every time you need a new spring hat, he will have spent all the money on new hair-growers and new scalp-treatments, none of which will do any good anyway, and you will spend the rest of your life in penury and sorrow. You will never have the companionship you hoped for. Every time you need him to mend a chair, or repair the porch, or unstick a stuck window, he will be upstairs in the bathroom, gloomily rubbing things on his head. No, this man is not for you.

Be on guard against a man with a heavy beard. You must be constantly on the alert for this as during the period of the courtship he may willingly shave twice a day in order to deceive you. However, once married this will lead to endless trouble. He will no longer shave willingly twice a day, but will grumble and complain and make a horrible fuss about it. And you don't want a man who will grumble and complain and fuss—that's *your* department. He will never listen sympathetically to your troubles about getting your hair to look right if he's brooding about having to shave again before you go out. If he has a heavy beard, forget him now.

Above all, make sure that this man has good ordinary feet that wear, comfortably, an ordinary average-size shoe. Should he ever once, during the period of courtship, mention any difficulty in buying shoes, or should you notice that he has new shoes rather often, or should you observe that he wiggles his toes a lot, give him the brush. The problem here is two-fold. It is worse than baldness and a heavy beard combined, as he will both complain *and* spend all your money. He will keep trying new lasts and new leathers and new styles and new shoe stores, but alas, his feet will still hurt. Every night he will want to put on his slippers and put his feet up, and *you* want him to put up the storm windows. No, this will never do. So if he has long, delicate, slender-boned feet, count him out as a possible mate. You've got foot troubles of your own, and you always need a large wardrobe of shoes.

Some faults which you may find in a man that may seem to be troublesome can be remedied. By you. After the marriage has taken place. If he is terribly fussy about his shirts, for instance, don't worry. He is safe to marry anyway, as you can then take the steps outlined in Chapter Three.

You want this man, with whom you are going to have to live for a long time, to be very careful about money. You don't want to be chained to a mad spend-thrift who'll go off and buy himself cameras and watches and fishing rods and overcoats. You want the kind of man who'll wait to buy a new overcoat till you're really certain that the old one can't possibly get through another year as the moth holes have now gone all the way through the material. On the other hand, you don't want to spend your life married to some terrible miser who'll suggest that you wear that passé opossum one more year. So be on your guard here, and choose wisely. The husband, that is. Not the fur coat. The fur coat you should choose extravagantly. Who knows when you'll get another?

Check up on this man's income. Many foolish young girls are hesitant about this as they think it isn't nice to talk about money. But you cannot be too careful as your entire future happiness depends on it, perhaps more than any other thing. The rule to follow here is simple. Emblazon it on your shield and burn it into your memory. Money may not be everything, but after all, you don't want to spend the rest of your life doing *housework*, do you?